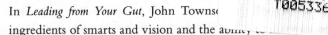

In *Leading from Your Gut*, John Towns[e] ingredients of smarts and vision and the ab[ility to] more intangible quality of "gut," which is essential to actually accomplishing change that lasts. Hands down, my new favorite leadership book.

Elisa Morgan, MDiv, speaker; author,*The Beauty of Broken, The Prayer Coin*; cohost, *Discover the Word*, www.discovertheword.org; President Emerita, MOPS International, www.mops.org

I mean—honestly—reading what Dr. Townsend writes gives you a totally unfair advantage over everyone else. In *Leading from Your Gut*, Dr. Townsend—once again—helps us optimize our lives for personal and professional success. Read this one, now, and all of it because you need it.

Johnnie Moore, founder, The KAIROS Company; recipient of the "Medal of Valor," Simon Wiesenthal Center

John takes the leader to a new level of performance by demonstrating there is more to leadership than traditional thinking would suggest. John's principles take you to your logic and your gut, and they work; apply them, and you will become a more impactful and fulfilled leader.

Greg Campbell, former executive vice president, Coldwell Banker

Learning what motivates your leadership decisions "from your gut" will help you make the good ones and, just as important, avoid the bad ones. This book is an intriguing and thought-provoking analysis of effective leadership.

Gary Daichendt, former executive vice president for worldwide operations, Cisco Systems

Just another leadership book? *Not hardly!* John Townsend challenges us to look beyond the usual sources as we develop *leadership skill.* Describing the key tools in producing exceptional leaders, John presents a compelling case for going "beyond reason" to acquire all the essential components of a good leader. His thorough assessment of the importance of values, thoughts, emotions, relationships, and transformation is productive and thought provoking. Why would we settle for anything less than a complete toolbox?

Bill Yingling, former chairman and CEO, Thrifty Corp.

Dr. John Townsend's new book, *Leading from Your Gut*, debuts at the perfect moment, amidst the bedlam of our turbulent times. It presents a magnificent challenge to both seasoned and aspiring leaders to approach leadership from a fresh and redemptive perspective, pivoting on the too long glossed over intangibles—values, thoughts, emotions, and relationships.

Allan O. Hunter Jr., cofounder, Rent.com

John reminds us we are in the *people* business. Many in leadership roles tend to ignore their emotions or assume their influence is negative and a threat to their effectiveness. John presents a compelling case for learning to recognize, integrate, and leverage our emotions for greater leadership results.

Fred Gladney, owner, Trinity Consulting; and former director and general manager of services, Compaq

LEADING FROM YOUR GUT

Other Books by
Dr. John Townsend

Boundaries

The Entitlement Cure

Who's Pushing Your Buttons?

Handling Difficult People

How to Have that Difficult Conversation You've Been Avoiding

LEADING FROM YOUR GUT

HOW YOU CAN SUCCEED BY HARNESSING THE POWER OF YOUR VALUES, FEELINGS, & INTUITION

A completely revised edition of *Leadership Beyond Reason*

DR. JOHN TOWNSEND

ZONDERVAN

Leading from Your Gut
Copyright © 2018 by John Townsend
A completely revised edition of *Leadership Beyond Reason*

Requests for information should be addressed to:
Zondervan, *3900 Sparks Dr. SE, Grand Rapids, Michigan 49546*

ISBN 978-0-310-35011-8 (softcover)

ISBN 978-0-310-35012-5 (ebook)

Published in association with Yates & Yates, LLP, www.yates2.com.

Art direction: Curt Diepenhorst
Interior design: Denise Froehlich

First printing April 2018/Printed in the United States of America

To my parents John and Rebecca Townsend, who both passed away during the writing of this book. There is no way to thank you enough for the many years of love, nurturance, and development you built into my life;

and

To everyone who aspires to be the best possible leader.

ACKNOWLEDGMENTS

Thanks to the following people who helped, in many ways, to bring about this book:

Sealy Yates and Mike Salisbury, my literary agents: You helped create the big picture of a leadership book that dealt with the internal world and partnered with me in its formation. Thanks for your help in pushing the envelope.

David Morris, vice president and publisher for Zondervan: I have so appreciated your "can do" spirit and all your negotiating efforts in helping this new book become a Zondervan product.

Sandy Vander Zicht and Christine Anderson, editors for Zondervan: Thanks for being partners in the process of crafting and honing this book to be engaging and helpful.

The team heading up the Townsend Leadership Group: Karen Bergstrom, Dennis Del Valle, Pamela Flores, Christine Ledet, Elaine Morris, Leah Nelson, and Patrick Sells, including each of the directors, consultants, and coaches, as well as the current and alum members of TLP. Thanks so much for your character and competencies in what you do as leaders worldwide.

Scott Makin, Doug Grove, the faculty, fellows, team, and all of the students and alums at the Townsend Institute for Leadership and Counseling: You are all so inspirational in your consuming quest for holistic excellence.

Maureen Price, executive director of Growth Skills Foundation, and her team, Jodi Coker, Lisa Leets, and the workshop facilitators: You continually shepherd and improve the workshops in ways that create growth and change for so many leaders.

Dr. Henry Cloud: It has been a great experience conceptualizing and working on the issues of leadership and the psychological world. Thank you for who you are as a person and as a friend.

Christine Ames and Vanessa Sedano, my assistants: Thanks for keeping me as organized as much as I will allow it ☺.

The Tuesday men's group: for being "there" with and for me for all these years.

My advisory board: for providing many hours of high-level grace and truth to keep me focused and targeted on the goals.

My clients and friends in leadership who have provided so many case studies of how to Lead from Your Gut: what examples you are of how to do it right!

Barbi, my wife: for your unflagging love and support, and for always being my first editor.

Ricky and Benny Townsend, my sons: it has been awesome seeing you now take your own places as experts and leaders in your professional worlds.

CONTENTS

Chapter 1

HARNESSING YOUR INTUITION

The board of a large manufacturing company had asked me to work with their leadership team on improving performance. When I met with the team, I interviewed them one-on-one and also rounded out the picture by asking them for feedback on each other.

I quickly found out that the CEO, Alex, was a major concern to both the team and the board. Four years previously, he had been promoted internally from his position as CFO, a role in which he had excelled. He was brilliant in complex analytics and financial formulas. However, since taking the helm of the company, Alex had made a few costly missteps—mistakes that went well beyond the normal learning curve of a new leader.

The most obvious misstep was committing significant resources to a new product line, which ended up not working out and damaging the company's financial state. Being a data-driven person, Alex had analyzed the metrics of the line and had created positive projections for its success. On a strictly numerical level, it should have all worked out. However, his key clients and his team didn't think the product line was a fit for the company—it was too extreme a departure from their core business. And, as Alex himself later told me, he'd had the same "gut" thought, though it was not backed up by his projections. However, the data trumped the gut and he pulled the trigger, leading to a problem the company then had to dig its way out of.

When I asked Alex how he viewed his decision-making process, he said, "I think it's pretty simple. I made a 100 percent data-driven decision. And I remember feeling anxious that we were too far away from our core. But I didn't trust that anxiety. I thought it was weakening my logical thought processes. So I didn't pay enough attention to what I and others were thinking and feeling about it, and it ended up being a bad call."

This was the point at which I began to work with Alex and his team. Obviously, the analytic emphasis of the company wasn't the broken part—that was strong and sound. It was the "inner voice" part I wanted to dig into. *Why did Alex not listen to his gut, and to the input of those around him?* If we could get to the bottom of that question, I felt confident we could turn things around—for both the company and for Alex. Alex could become a great senior-level leader if he could learn to draw on internal data as well as external data.

And that, quite simply, is the premise of this book. Great leaders succeed by harnessing the power of both the external world and the internal world. You, as a leader, are probably more trained, prepared, and experienced in the external world than you are in the internal one. Most likely, you are able to amass large amounts of valuable information from reports, research, journals, and input from colleagues. And you need that information; it is critical to your success as a leader. At the same time, you also need access to data within you that is just as valuable and helpful to how you lead, relate to others, and make decisions.

This book is designed to help you understand and access what is inside you—your intuition or your gut—so you can use that internal data to help you succeed.

Reason, in the sense of using rationality, logic, and objective sources of information, is clearly a necessary core component of leadership. No person of influence can function at high levels without it. However, there are also important leadership aspects that transcend pure reasoning. They are subjective, internal, and experiential. These *intuitive* aspects of leadership are not infallible, but they are highly significant and valuable. Leaders who want to keep growing, to be equipped and empowered for the next level, must know how to utilize all the resources and tools available to them. This is what separates the great leaders from the good ones.

What Intuition IS—And What It Isn't

There are several ways to describe and recognize intuition. Sometimes it is referred to as your subjective, internal, or inner world. However, at the end of the day, it is simply *your immaterial life*. Within you are values, thoughts, emotions, and passions. They cannot be seen or touched because they are not physical. But they are real, they exist, they are an essential part of you—and they will serve you well if you honor and develop them.

Some theorists define intuition as the ability to understand something without using conscious reasoning. My own definition is broader. I see intuition as *the capacity to make decisions based on integrating objective and subjective truth*. That is, when we access both internal and external information, we have a much more accurate understanding of reality, and a greater ability to make the right decisions. Thus, intuitive leaders—those who lead from the gut—pay attention not just to numbers and research, but also to their own heart, as well as other internal realities we'll cover in this book.

I believe Jesus was referring to a similar dynamic when he said, "Love the Lord your God with all your *heart* and with all your *soul* and with all your *mind*" (Matthew 22:37, emphasis added). When we integrate all of ourselves in seeking him, our lives work better. In the same way, when we integrate all the avenues of truth we can access into our leadership, we can make much better decisions.

There are a few other terms that can be confused with this understanding of intuition, and it may help to clarify these:

- *Instinct:* Instinct is an innate, inborn behavior pattern that does not have its basis in learning. For example, birds build nests without seeing how their parents did it. And I have seen leaders act to protect their people without a thought for themselves, as a parent acts on instinct to save her child. A good illustration of this is a business owner friend who, hearing that an employee's child was very sick, ran out of a board meeting and went straight to the hospital to help.
- *Impulse:* An impulse is an abrupt emotion that is strong enough to drive a behavior without thinking about it. For example, rather than thinking through the source of the frustration, a leader may impulsively lash out.

- *Spiritualization:* Spiritualization is the tendency to use one's faith to avoid making tough decisions. It can be driven by a fear of making mistakes, a fear of conflict, or even by laziness. For example, a CEO might say, "I'm waiting on the Lord for a leading about whether or not to acquire that company," when the truth is that the CEO is avoiding time-consuming due diligence work or potential conflict with other leaders.

Intuition, as I use it with my clients, differs from instinct, impulse, and spiritualization. It is hard work that requires a lot of thinking, feeling, and talking things through, and then allowing all those aspects of decision-making to shake hands with one another. But time and time again, I have found that the best leaders make the best choices by engaging in this approach.

In this book, we'll explore five key aspects that shape your intuitive world—values, thoughts, emotions, relationships, and transformation—and how you can use them not only to make better decisions but to significantly impact your leadership for the long haul. When used the right way, your gut intuition—all these internal aspects of who you are—will become a vital and essential part of your leadership repertoire.

How Intuitive Is Your Leadership?

If I asked you to assess the level of intuition in your leadership on a scale of one to ten (1 low, 10 high), what number would you choose? Go ahead and write it down. Then use the assessment that follows to help you gain additional insights about where you are in this dimension of your leadership.

Next to each of the statements below, write the number 1 if your response is yes, and 0 if your response is no.

_____ Overall, the leadership training I have received has placed as much emphasis on the value of my inner world and personal experience as it has on my external competencies and skills.

_____ I have made "gut" leadership decisions that did not seem to be logical at the time, but ultimately proved to be the best decision.

_____ I have ignored my gut in making decisions and later realized it was a mistake.

_____ Based on my experience of emotions in leadership, I would say that paying attention to my feelings routinely helps me to reach my goals.

_____ I esteem intuition (internal information) as much as objective information when considering decisions.

_____ If asked, I could describe how I intentionally make use of intuition (my inner world) in leadership and also list several recent examples.

_____ Even when I am under pressure to produce results, I rely on both externals and internals—hard facts and intuition—to implement strategies and navigate professional relationships.

_____ I trust the power of my emotions as much as I trust the power of my intellect to help me make good leadership decisions.

_____ I routinely reflect on my core values, which means I rarely make on-the-fly decisions that conflict with my values.

_____ I spend as much of my time and energy on personal growth and transformation as I do in developing other areas of life that are important to me and impact my leadership effectiveness (for example, professional training/education, physical health and exercise, etc.).

_____ Total

Briefly review your responses and add up your total. How does the total compare to the number you wrote down before the assessment? Is it higher, lower, about the same?

If your responses to these statements landed your total in the lower numbers, don't be discouraged. That is actually normal for most leaders. And there are some good reasons for this. You have a responsibility to create good outcomes and to help people achieve them. The outcomes are generally measurable, such as profits, customer service ratings, attendance figures, or some other growth metric. Because leaders are evaluated in objective and measurable ways, you may tend to look only at the facts to help you achieve your goals.

The process is similar to the outcome, in that sense. You trust what you see and read, things that can be proven and measured. For example, a profit-and-loss statement is reliable. It has the facts. The information is there, in black and white, and it does not change. It is hard data. However, hard data rarely tells the whole story, and if you choose to ignore the soft data—your intuition—*you do so at your peril.* As we will see, leaders who don't pay attention to their inner world miss a great deal of additional data, ranging from the gut data Alex ignored about the new product line, to the ability to relate to and understand those you work with and lead. Disregarding this essential information can not only negatively affect the quality of your judgments and decisions today but also undermine your long-term leadership impact.

There is another reason most leaders' responses to the assessment statements tend to be more zeros than ones. It is the belief that the subjective world slows you down, blunts your edge, gets you off focus, or makes you too touchy-feely to be respected. You become concerned that *inner* matters will distract you from achieving your goals and mission or make you look weak. You begin to think that attending to your inner data will cloud rather than clarify your judgment and ultimately make you less decisive. And there is actually some logic to this thinking. If you, the leader, are to run ahead of your competition or meet the next challenging objective, doesn't the process of stopping to see what you feel, sense, believe, or think slow things down? In the short term, certainly. Paying attention to your inside world takes some amount of time. But in the long term, I can promise you that learning to harness your internal data not only brings a high return on that investment, it also helps others to trust you as a person, creates a higher success rate of great decisions, and ultimately drives your organization's mission in the right direction. That is one reason for the popularity of leadership books on values, emotional intelligence,[1] and personal growth. The internal supports the external—and it produces results.

Scan Your Inner World

The simplest way to understand how you can put information from your inner world to work in leadership is to consider how you already do that with information from external sources. Most leaders regularly read the newspaper or get the news online or on TV. You subscribe to magazines and journals in your area of specialty. You receive reports and e-mails on your organization. Leaders are information junkies, and they need to be. You are constantly scanning the horizon to look at trends, the future, opportunities, threats, and people. Similarly, you also need to be able to do an *interior scan*—that is, you need the skill to access what's going on inside you, regularly and on demand, so you can tap into that source as well. One of the major goals of this book is to help you hone the ability to scan the different aspects of your inner world. The more information you have about your inner world, generally the better you can decide and lead.

Not only that, but those you lead also have an inner world, a subjective experience. They have feelings, creativity, and their own thoughts. Their lives also have areas that are intuitive and beyond reason. As a leader, you must connect with their insides to develop them as people and contributors. This cannot be done if you are not in the process yourself. All of us have had the experience of being led by someone who may have been competent and principled but was simply clueless about subjective matters. You may have respected and liked the person, but you probably also found that he or she could not understand nuances of what you were trying to say, or differences you had, or your emotional experiences. And this lack of understanding was probably more than frustrating; it likely didn't move the mission of the organization along. Leaders who can learn to understand what their gut is telling them, as Alex did in time, are better able to understand the fears of those they lead. As you scan your inner world, you help others scan theirs as well.

Not a 180 but an Addition

If you regularly read books on leadership and business, you are probably aware that there is a tendency for authors to present their approach as a new paradigm that revolutionizes everything that has come before, so the new book will be a 180-degree change in direction for the leader and the organization. That is not the case for this book.

Though there are classics in leadership literature, must-reads for any leader, I shy away from 180-degree proclamations. Leadership has been studied and researched by many competent people for many years. I think most leadership books that make substantial contributions build on what has already been done well. They add to the leader's repertoire of abilities and skills. They remove some unhelpful ways of thinking, conceptualizing, relating, and behaving. But they don't remove the good stuff.

I want you to continue your own leadership training in this very significant aspect of the inner world and its contents. The principles described here are compatible with sound leadership theories and practices that already work for you. So look at this book as helping you to achieve great results by going deeper into what is already inside you.

Because of the importance of reason in successful leadership, part 2 will explain how leaders can improve and better utilize their thoughts and the thinking process.

Why You Became a Leader

Let's clarify who this book is for, as *leader* is a broad term. Basically, this material is designed for you if you are engaged in *influencing others to achieve results and goals*. To influence someone is to have an effect on them. To make a difference. Much has been written about the power of influence, and this gives room for all sorts of people to qualify as leaders. Here are some examples:

- Corporate executives and managers
- Small business owners
- Physicians and those in the medical field
- Psychologists and those in the helping professions
- Pastors and ministry leaders
- Small group leaders and facilitators
- Teachers

It is a broad net. Effective leadership creates a setting in which people live better and are more productive, effective, creative, resourceful, and higher functioning. More than that, leaders make their organization one with better results.

You most likely became a leader for some reason that was beyond reason. Most of us don't start out in life thinking, *I don't know what I want to be good at, but I want to lead some people.* In fact, that could be an indication of a psychological problem. It's more likely that something inside you gradually came alive the more you grew, learned, and interacted with people. In other words, your inner world led you to leadership. For example:

- You liked working in teams and people told you, "You're good at motivating people."
- You had a vision to build an organization and realized you would need to recruit, train, and keep good people around you.
- You were an expert in some competency field and felt that it wasn't enough, that you wanted to reach out and connect with others in addition to your expertise.
- You wanted to make a difference in some specific area of life or work, and you loved seeing people grow and change in that difference.

You probably would not have taken on the hard work, pressure, and demands of leadership had not your world beyond reason been moving and pushing you. It informs us, drives us, keeps us going in tough times, gives us wisdom and discernment, and connects us to others. It is often the part of us that first resonated with the possibility that we might be a good leader doing a worthwhile endeavor.

Keeping Your Eye on the Ball

I consulted many friends in business and leadership during the process of writing this book, and they have all said something like this: "Show the reader how harnessing the power of the inner world brings results." Leaders are under tremendous pressure to bring about outcomes and results. The bottom line belongs to the leader, whether it is revenues, profits, production, lives changed, or number of meetings. Any way you look at it, leaders must keep their eye on the ball.

Dealing with the subjective world has everything to do with producing good results. It is an essential aspect of your own success and your ability to help others succeed. This book is not some kind of exercise in self-actualization that I hope will one day in the distant future make a difference. When you finish reading this book, my goal is for you to say, "I not only understand myself better, but I can also see leadership results from what I have learned."

Whatever leadership niche you are in, from the corporate world to leading a small group, you will discover aspects of your interior world that will come to your aid. You were designed with both an external world and an inner world, and they work well together. Accessing both of these areas will take a little knowledge and a little work, but it will help you be the leader you want to be. So we will begin with the first and most foundational aspect of the inner world of the leader: your values.

PART I

VALUES

THE BEDROCK OF LEADERSHIP

A client and friend of mine, Dave Lindsey, founded and ran a large home security company for many years. Dave's organization has experienced enormous growth over the years. One of his core tenets, and one he often speaks about to leadership groups, is this: "Businesses don't grow, people do." The implication is that when you invest in the growth of your people, you are investing in the business. Dave then follows that statement with this one: "Work on yourself more than you work on the business." In other words, prioritize personal growth and self-improvement.

Think about this for a minute. If you consider Dave's statements from a strictly logical and analytic point of view, they might sound a bit crazy. Wouldn't this sort of approach lead people to lose their alignment to the organization's vision, not to mention their focus on job performance? Yet, year after year, Dave's employees have driven the organization to greater growth and success.

Dave has also consistently lived out these values in leading his company. It has worked, and is a powerful example of how important it is to think through your values so you can use them to become the effective and intuitive leader you want to be. Here are two conclusions I draw from Dave's story, and that of other leaders I have worked with:

1. *It is important to have values.*
2. *It is important to have the right values.*

I will add a third one to that, which we will examine in the next chapter:

3. *It is important for your values to be from inside you.*

Your values are a part of your internal DNA. That is, they are true and absolute for you, whether or not you think about them. Your values are simply aspects of reality that are guides for you. That is what discovering your values is all about, thinking through the process of determining what guidelines and principles will order our steps. Values are about what is right and what matters.

Your inside life is the repository of your values, so we begin with values because most of your life springs from them. Your values are the bedrock of your identity. And your leadership, as well as your life, will reflect your values, for good or for bad. Some people are in prison right now because their values guided them to that end. And others are succeeding beyond their wildest dreams for the same reason.

Chapter 2

WHAT ARE VALUES?

When I am training a group of leaders, I often begin with this question, "Okay, how many of you can state your organization's core values, the ones that are on your website?" The great majority will be able to recite them on the spot. They say things like:

- Integrity
- Excellence
- Great culture
- Customer-centric

Then I say, "That's great! Now, how many of you can state your personal core values?" Most of the time, the room will go silent, or a few people will scratch their heads. Sometimes a brave soul will say something like, "Love God and people."

The room goes silent because personal values tend to be something most of us haven't thought through clearly enough. But here is the point for leaders: *The internal values of the leader must cascade into the organizational values of the company, not the reverse.* You have a thing called a life. Hopefully your life is driven by your values. And your organization is part of your life, not all of it. Your life is the horse, and your work is the cart, or that's how it's supposed to be. So it's worth working out, imprinting on your brain, and then living out what your own internal values are. And that leads well into being the intuitive, integrated leader you were designed to be.

I am not trying to shame anyone when I ask these questions during a leadership training. In fact, years ago, I came to all of this the hard way myself—after I had started a second business and had to go backward to get my own personal values work done. At the end of that process, I identified my own seven[1] core values, which I describe at the end of this part of the book. The process was challenging but has been so worth it, especially in terms of having a congruent life—one in which my work values are consistent with my life values.

The word *value* basically means "worth." A value is something that you determine has a great deal of worth. Jesus said, "For where your treasure is, there your heart will be also" (Matthew 6:21), which is about values. What you value as your treasure is connected to what is inside your very heart.

So your values are those realities you believe in at the deepest level, so much so that they dictate your decisions and your leadership—for good or for not-so-good. Whether they be about the company or about your life, research has shown that values are foundational in staying true and focused on the right things, using them as "north stars" to make the best decisions. So this section will help you clarify what you believe is most important for yourself and for your organization.

Internal Values First, Organizational Values Second

Why do I believe it's a mistake to come up with organizational values without first having done the work of determining your personal values? Because internal values will always trump organizational values. Perhaps you'll recognize one of these scenarios . . .

- Matt is a founding partner in a two-year-old tech start-up. Although the future of the company depends on creativity and continuous innovation, Matt is a micromanager. His ability to be hands on with everything was necessary when the company started, but now it's a problem. Even though the organization says it values allowing choice and giving freedom to others, Matt fails to recognize how his high control value undermines the organization's innovation and creativity values.

- Sandra owns a small IT company whose website states one of its values as "honesty and truthfulness in all matters." Yet, she is terribly conflict-avoidant and doesn't want to hurt people's feelings, so she postpones the tough talks with employees who are not performing or relating well. Though it was hard for her to admit it, her internal value of "keeping the peace" trumps her stated organizational values, and does so to the detriment of her company. People have trust issues with her because she isn't forthright, and they also resent individuals who disregard corporate values and practices because they know she won't confront them.
- Robert runs a precision manufacturing company which has little margin for error in producing quality products. The corporate value is, "At the end of the day, it's only about performance." It's a good value, but one that Robert actually "violates" in a positive way. Time and time again, I have witnessed him supporting a struggling employee who was not performing, a decision based more on his compassion and care for the person than corporate values or the bottom line. When I asked Robert about this, he said, "I probably should change the value statement on the website. It's true that we are all about performance, but there are times that you just have to help someone."

Based on these examples, it's not hard to see how internal values trump organizational values, but what if you're not the senior leader in an organization? What if you don't have any say in the organizational values and you aren't in a position to revise them? If this is your situation, you can still use your internal values to help and support the organization. Healthy values always work together. Also, use your internal values to determine if the organization is a good fit for you, and vice versa. For example, if one of your internal values is about relationship, and the "people factor" is not an important part of the organization's DNA, you are now aware of that and can consider whether you should be there in the first place, or at least how to deal with that difference.

So the order is internal values first, organizational values second. The intuitive, integrated leader is constantly aware of this priority.

Four Characteristics of From-Your-Core Values

In chapter 3 we'll take a closer look at the sources of values and how you can identify your own, but for now, let's assume that you have already spent time determining both your internal and organizational values. There is another step to consider, and that is *whether or not your values are from your core—really and authentically from you.* I call them *from-your-core values* to differentiate them from the overused *core values* term. The first is more personal, and the second tends to refer to the conceptual.

How can you know if your stated values are ones that are actually part of who you are? I have seen many leaders who considered their organizational values in some sort of consultation or task setting and were diligent about it. And the result was a document, an e-mail, a poster, or a tagline of things everyone signed off on. But at the end of the day, no one really and truly changed their behavior based on these stated values. Nor would they think about them when faced with an opportunity or a problem. These values weren't part of the fabric of the leader's heart. They were helpful and potentially valuable, but they weren't truly internalized, and so they had no meaningful impact.

I was friends with a group of people in a media services corporation who suffered the consequences of such not-core values. The CEO, Randy, was a very competent, creative, and positive person. He had come from another industry in the corporate environment and was doing a good job of adapting his expertise to the media world. One of Randy's strengths was that he didn't pretend to be perfect. He admitted when he was wrong, didn't hide mistakes, and was gracious when other people struggled. He talked about having a high value for authenticity, and people were drawn to his vulnerability. He readily laughed at his mistakes, and people in his organization felt safe and comfortable around him.

However, it turned out that Randy's authenticity value had limits. To live out his high value for authenticity, he needed to consistently take responsibility for whatever it was he was being authentic about. So his ability to admit his mistakes was a good thing. But true authenticity also means doing whatever is required to address and resolve the situation. And that's where Randy's authenticity value fell short.

As it turns out, he made an error in judgment that cost the organization a great deal of money. He did not take into account some market shifts. That happens. It was a big deal but not so big that the organization wanted to let him go. They were willing to work with him, make the necessary corrections, and move on. Lesson learned. However, in order to do this, the board of directors began some very frank and direct talks with Randy so that everyone could do the right surgery, be on the same page, and resolve the issue.

After the second meeting, Randy resigned. He felt that the board was too harsh and unfair in their evaluations. I knew the board members and had heard their side of the situation. It sounded like while they were very honest, they were also on Randy's side and tried to be balanced. This was Randy's first serious leadership mistake, and they were shocked by his reaction. With his previous *misdemeanor* offenses, Randy would admit his errors, people would be compassionate, and everyone would put them behind him. But this time, when his error in judgment was categorized a *felony,* his values failed.

Randy's resignation revealed that his value for authenticity was half-hearted, not really driven from his core. It looked good on paper and in small matters, but he readily set it aside when abiding by it involved difficulty and confrontation. Randy was authentic to the point of admitting small problems; however, he did not have the stomach to look at his major failures. Instead, he felt misunderstood and persecuted when others pointed out serious problems even when they wanted to help him.

This is what I mean when I say your inner life—and especially the values that drive your choices—matters so much for your leadership. If you want to take your leadership to the next level, your values have to be *from your core*—that is, from the deepest part of who you really are. They have to be so rooted in who you are that you won't set them aside, especially when the stakes are high.

So how can you know what your from-your-core values are? I've described four key characteristics below. Before you read through them, jot down a few phrases about what you think some of your values are, or pull out your list of values if you have one. Then keep these values in mind as you consider each of the four characteristics. This will help you to clarify what your values might be and also to assess how "from-your-core" they actually are.

This applies to you whether or not you have actually crafted your organizational values. If you are in a company, organization, or church that already has a stated set of values, use the four characteristics to determine how you relate to those values. If you are not in alignment with the values, it will help you determine if the problem is that you haven't yet "bought in," haven't thought them through, or actually do not share the values.

1. When Your Values Aren't Lived Out, It Bothers You

If your values are from your core, you notice when they aren't honored and executed, especially in a business or organization setting. Not only do you notice, but you are bothered by it. A values violation doesn't just register as a minor blip; it sets off an internal alarm that says, *This isn't okay with me!* You can't just pass it off.

For example, suppose fairness is a personal value; you want to see people treated justly in your group. Then say your direct report comes to you with a complaint about another individual and neglects to go to that person first. That is gossip. It hurts people, and it isn't fair treatment. If fairness is a deep value, you will be bothered by this even though the information about the offending individual could be useful to you. But the bigger picture is what you respond to, and your sense of being disturbed is a good thing.

A few years ago, I attended an election-year fund-raising event. The speaker, a well-known political leader, was talking about the presidential candidates, and he went over the positions they were taking on various issues. He also talked about the dilemma most of us face in an election: we don't agree with everything any one candidate says, so how do we decide for whom to vote? Then he made a values *aha!* statement that stuck with me: "There are some issues I don't have to agree with and will still vote for a candidate. But other issues are so important to me that if I voted for a person who disagreed with my position on them, *I wouldn't know who I am anymore.*" What did this man respond to? It was the awareness that some hills are not worth dying on, and some are.

That is what I mean by "when your values aren't lived out, it bothers you." Compromise and negotiation are valuable in leadership. But when it comes to values, you want to always know who you are.

Some people can be faced with values dilemmas and not be bothered. They quickly make a decision, count the losses, and move on. This is not a good sign. It could mean that they haven't really delved into the value, and it's still an idea, but no more. Or it could mean that they think more in terms of what author James O'Toole calls *contingency*, meaning that the values aren't universal but relative to the situation.[2] These people believe they can change the rules of integrity if the situation warrants it, which is a serious problem. Finally, it could mean that they have a character problem, and instead of seeking consistency and integration of their values, they compartmentalize incompatible realities. They aren't upset when values are violated. This requires more work if that is the case.

2. When Your Values Are Lived Out, You Know Why

This is the flip side of the previous characteristic. If your values are from the core, you readily notice when they *are* being lived out. And you not only notice, you understand why and how the values operate. In other words, there is a direct and observable correlation between the value and the health of your organization. It may not come out in the next day, but it will come out eventually, and be noticeable, for better or worse.

Let's revisit the previous scenario—about the direct report with a complaint against a coworker—but with one difference. This time, the direct report comes to you after he has done the hard work of confronting the offending individual. In this case, the offender was defensive or nonresponsive. So now your direct report asks you for help, as you are the legitimate next step in the conflict resolution protocol. You know that it was difficult for him to attempt to talk to the individual, but approaching the offending party first was the right thing to do. And you know it was not only the right thing for the organization, but it bodes well for your team's success. People do better when they know they are treated fairly. And people in your organization trust you and your best practices more because you play by your own rules. You understand the "why" of the reality that the company will run better in both performance and culture, due to the value being expressed and lived out correctly. The "why" connects the dots between action and consequence, between what the Bible calls sowing and reaping (Galatians 6:7).

So when you see your values lived out, you understand why and how it impacts the health of the organization and your ability to lead effectively. As a result, you know that, as my friend Dr. Henry Cloud says, "The good guys win."[3]

3. You Experience Your Values More than Remind Yourself about Them

When your values are wholehearted—internally based—you may not even think about them explicitly. They have become so ingrained that they are just part of how you naturally think, relate, and lead. It's certainly helpful to review your list of values and continue updating and improving them. But when they are the right ones, you don't have to keep reading them as a reminder. Instead, you routinely experience them—you *live what you value.*

Here's a recent example. I was working with a pastor who had a rocky relationship with one of his colleagues. He had disagreed with a decision his colleague had made, and in response, the other pastor had accused him of mistreating him and began an underground campaign against the first pastor. The conflict was threatening to tear the church apart. People were taking sides. After carefully listening to information from both men, I believed the first pastor was in the right and the second one was clearly wrong. I went to the first one and said, "I believe you in this situation. But I think you should call the other pastor and offer to reconcile somehow. I know he should call you first, but because he feels like you've treated him wrong, he won't. If you want to solve this problem, I think it's your move."

I knew that this pastor had a high value on ownership—that is, taking responsibility for his life and his outcomes. The man didn't hesitate. He immediately picked up the phone and made the call. He humbled himself to being the one who *owned* the problem and reached out to the other pastor even though he had been wronged. The second man eventually left, but his exit was not nearly as traumatic to the church as it could have been.

I want to focus on the *immediate* part of the first pastor's response. I had expected him to say something like, "It's *his* problem; why doesn't he come to me?" He could have, except that he was living out the ownership value from his core. He did not have to pull out an index card with his list of values and review what he should do. There was no need to. His internal world was so transformed by his ownership value that it became his default mode, even in a difficult situation. He didn't grit his teeth and try hard to go the extra mile with ownership, he simply responded from who he authentically is—as a person and as a leader. That's a big part of what it means to lead with intuition, with all of yourself.

4. You Make a Direct Connection Between Values and Good Outcomes

Let's return to the big idea of this book: leading with intuition—with all you are in your "insides"—ultimately produces better results in your leadership. So as you work on your organization, develop your people, and pursue your goals, you are able to see how the right values are essential in bringing about the fruit you want. They shape everything from your conversations and the way you relate to people, to your strategic plans and decisions—and maybe even how you respond to recognition. I recently complimented a friend who is part owner of a thriving commercial building renovation organization. He had told me how he had entered the business at nineteen with nothing, apprenticing himself to an older man. He had truly begun at the lowest rung of the ladder. Then, over time, he worked hard, made sure he had a great product, set up effective systems and processes, kept great relationships, treated his employees right, and eventually negotiated a partnership with his owner. Now in his forties, he is quite successful.

I was impressed by his work and his achievements. When I complimented him, this is how he described the key to his success. "I have tried to be aware that there's a lot I don't know," he said, "so I always need to listen and learn." Do you see what he did there? As soon as I complimented him, he made a direct connection between his values and his good outcomes—a key indication that his values are deep and wholehearted.

When great leaders analyze their wins and their losses, they spend considerable time exploring how those outcomes were driven by either adhering to or veering away from the compass of their values. They never forget the importance of the North Star of values.

It Makes a Difference

Your core values are the "gut" of your organization. As you think in terms of your values, and use them intentionally when you make a decision, you will find this increasingly becomes an automatic habit. One client I have been working with for years has become very predicable with this—in a good way. Back when we first started working together, we would meet to discuss an opportunity or a challenge, and he would describe the situation. Then I would ask how his values played into the process. After working together for a while, he would describe his situation and then launch straight into saying, "Of course, my next thought needs to be about how my values play into the process." It is now a seamless and intuitive part of his decision-making.

So take a moment now to list not only your organization's core values, but also to start a list of your personal core values. Notice how they relate and align, or to what extent they fail to align. The next chapter will help you take the next step in the process, which is to land your personal values.

Chapter 3

LANDING YOUR OWN VALUES

When I was in seminary, one of my professors, Dr. Charles Ryrie (author of the *Ryrie Study Bible*), told a memorable story about a conversation he had with one of his previous students.

"Can you give me a list of why you believe the Bible is true?" the student asked.

"I can," Dr. Ryrie said, "but I won't."

"Why not?" the student asked, a bit confused.

"It took me ten years to work out the reasons I believe the Bible is true," Ryrie said, "and I think about it, use it, and teach about it all the time. It impacts how I work. If I hand you a piece of paper with all of my reasons, what kind of passion will you have for teaching others? More than that, what kind of passion will those you teach have to teach it to others a generation down the line?"

This story illustrates an important principle: *For your values to matter, you must "own" and take responsibility for them.* We value things we have invested energy in because we have skin in the game. In order for your values to be more than a list on a wall plaque, you have to invest energy into figuring them out.

On the pages ahead, you'll work through a methodology to help you determine and "land" your own values, both personally and organizationally.

Personal Values

The most effective way to identify your values is to work from the inside out—to begin with your internal values, the "you" part of the equation.

You will find that your organizational values will then be much easier to determine.

Also, for now, don't set a limit on how many values you come up with—in fact, the more the better. When your list is pretty much exhausted through this methodology, you can pare it down to your top three to seven. This is the "blue sky" part of the process.

Step 1: Identify Your Aspirational Values

Begin by listing your *aspirational values*. Aspirational values are the truths you desire to live out, thus you "aspire" to them. You aspire to them because you haven't yet fully achieved them. Even so, they are principles you want to commit to and live out. The apostle Paul described one of his aspirational values when he wrote this about his desire for spiritual maturity and completeness: "Not that I have already obtained all this, or have already arrived at my goal, but I press on to take hold of that for which Christ Jesus took hold of me" (Philippians 3:12). In the same way, aspirational values inspire us, focus us, and give us a standard to shoot for. Here are some examples:

- Following God
- Prioritizing relationships
- Compassion for others
- Growing spiritually, personally, and emotionally
- Living a life of excellence
- Truthfulness and honesty
- Engaging in one's mission and purpose in life
- Learning to lead others well

Values are not something we create or make up on our own. Instead, we identify with and follow them. Values exist as universal truths, and are true whether or not we are aware of them or believe in them. Just as gravity causes things away from the earth to move back toward the earth, values are part of the fundamental rules of life.

People often think that setting out their personal values is a vague and onerous task, but I have found a simple, three-step way to make the work more doable and effective.

Set one primary aspirational value. Since God is the originator of all values in the universe, it simply makes sense for leaders who wish to work from an intuitive framework to begin with the following as their primary value: *Whatever God values, I will value.* Again, these are values we don't have to make up. In the Bible, God has already told us a number of things that matter to him. Here are some examples:

- *Love.* We must follow Jesus' commands to love God and love others (Matthew 22:36–40), which are the two highest values in God's kingdom. The apostle Paul provides additional teaching on what it means in practical terms to love others well (1 Corinthians 13:1–13).
- *Stewardship.* We are stewards of the earth and the tasks God gives us to do in the world. The first command God gives to Adam and Eve is to fill the earth, subdue it, and rule over it (Genesis 1:28).
- *Obedience.* We must follow God's commands. For example, the Ten Commandments (Exodus 20:1–17) list foundational directives to help us follow God and to treat each other well.
- *Wisdom.* We must learn to live well by pursuing wisdom. The book of Proverbs provides many principles about the value of skilled living.
- *Character.* We must grow in our ability to live an integrated life. The prophet Micah described the foundational requirements for character development this way: "To act justly and to love mercy and to walk humbly with your God" (Micah 6:8).
- *The gospel.* We must reach the world with the message of Christ, a charge often referred to as The Great Commission (Matthew 28:19–20).

Whichever value is "the one" for you, then review the rest in light of that one. As you reflect on this list, don't allow yourself to get overwhelmed by feeling like you have to have one "right" set of biblical values. There are hundreds—and the goal is to end up with a maximum of seven! Also, don't give in to all-or-nothing thinking, which says, "Now I'm leaving out the rest of the Bible." You are not. Whatever value number is for you, it's important to God and to you. But you have to stop somewhere, and I think you'll end up with a great direction in life—and in leadership—by keeping your list of foundational values down to somewhere between three and seven.

At the same time, remember that whatever the Bible says is most important is probably the most important for you. So keep that in mind as you craft your values list. For example, when I worked out my own internal value system, which is included at the end of this chapter, I was struck by the primacy of love in the Bible, and made sure it was primary in my own list.

So, the key standard to rely on as you begin with biblical values is this: *Whatever God values, I will value.* All your other aspirational values should serve and support this one.

Look to your aspirational role models. All of us have role models, mentors, and coaches who have inspired us to be more than we are. Mine the values of the people you trust, admire, and have been helped by. If they are alive, simply ask them: What are the foundational values you live by? If they are no longer living, review your history with them and determine the values you saw. If they are unknown to you personally, such as authors or great leaders in history, look to their writings or biographies to identify the values they embody. Add their values to your list.

For many years, I have had a board of advisers, several people who help me stay on track with my life, mission, career, and business areas. These are people who know me well, and give me guidance and accountability. They are also very successful and accomplished individuals in their own rights, so they have an experience base to speak from. I have picked up many aspirational values from my time with them, such as living with a vision, wisdom, authenticity, honesty, structure, and strategy. These helped form my thinking for my final internal values list.

Do a web search. Take advantage of the massive amounts of information available on the Internet. I have done many searches on values, and have discovered several that I might otherwise have overlooked. One was the value of creativity, for example. It didn't make the final cut, but it's on my longer list!

Step 2: Identify Your Observable Values

After identifying your aspirational values list, the next step is to identify your observable values, which I define as *that set of values I am already living out*. You don't have to go to an inspiring source to name these values; you just have to look at what is driving your current behaviors, interactions, and choices. You may not even be aware of your observable values, but something is influencing you to do what you are doing in your life and your leadership.

There are healthy observable values, and there are unhealthy ones. The healthy values are in line with what matters to God, and promote great growth, relationships, and productivity. In other words, they bear the right kind of fruit. The unhealthy values work against what God intends for you, and ultimately slow down or even derail your progress as a successful and fruit-bearing person.

Healthy observable values. Healthy observable values are basically you "at your best." That is, they are the principles that drive you to be the best person you can be, and to accomplish the best goals you can accomplish. You may not be aware of them, but they are there, promoting and influencing the right behaviors and attitudes.

For example, in the early stages of my work with Trent, a client of mine who runs an investment company with a large portfolio, I queried him about his own internal values. One thing I immediately noticed was that he is highly focused on keeping his priorities in mind at all times. This showed up in how attentive he is with his wife and kids, how he commits himself to his friends, how he serves at his church, and how disciplined he is in his exercise program (a lot more disciplined than I am). It is no stretch to see that his company is also one of clear priorities and focus. When I made these observations, he immediately said, "Yes, I place a high value on focusing on what is most important." Thus, his first internal observable value was stated and expressed.

Trent's observable value is good, it fits with other healthy values, and it helps create good fruit in his life. That's a healthy observable value. Look at your own life choices and see what the commonalities are. Ask those who know you well what they have observed in you as well. Add it all to your list.

Unhealthy observable values. Unfortunately, we can also be driven by values that aren't great, and don't work well for us or advance our mission in life. Until they are identified and resolved, these unhealthy values prevent us from being our best self. That's why taking the time to identify them is so important.

Matt and Sandra, the leaders we met in the previous chapter, are great examples of this. Matt's unhealthy value was "control at the expense of freedom," and Sandra's was "keep the peace at the expense of solving problems." Neither of them enjoyed identifying or owning up to those values, and both felt pretty yucky about themselves for a while. But they were committed to their own growth and the growth of their organizations, and they made great progress. Matt began trusting others and allowing mistakes, and Sandra began having frank and productive conversations that cleared the cultural air.

Once you've listed your unhealthy values, flip them around by identifying their opposite, and then add those healthy values to your list. What is the healthy value you want to live out to replace the unhealthy one? Matt flipped his unhealthy value of micromanaging into "trusting in the competency and character of others." Sandra flipped her unhealthy conflict avoidance value into "engaging in relational confrontations that solve problems and maintain the alliance." You can do the same for your own unhealthy values.

Don't let shame and guilt deter you from this important work. Focus on God's love and grace, and lean in to the people who are "for" you. They all want you to be the healthy, intuitive leader you were designed to be, and this is an essential step on the path to that goal. Bite the bullet and look at the patterns that have repeatedly led to regrettable choices for you.

Step 3: Pare Down Your List

By now, you should have way more than seven values—both aspirational and observable—maybe even a list numbering into three digits. Start whittling down the number. It is painful but necessary. Here are some tips to help.

Strike the obvious low priorities. These are the values that matter, but it's very clear to you that they aren't anywhere near the top seven. For example, "Keeping an organized office" is valuable, but it just doesn't make the cut.

Eliminate redundancies. Often you'll find values that are very close in meaning, so you can combine them or simply eliminate one. For example, "responsibility" and "ownership" could be collapsed into one value.

Sort the remaining values into "must-have" and "nice-to-have" columns. Your brain will start making distinctions for you.

Share your must-have column with a few trusted friends or colleagues and ask them to help you prune your favorites. Wise friends and colleagues can help you trim those important but nonessential favorites so you can narrow your focus down to your top seven values.

Once you have crafted, reviewed, and vetted your internal values list, you can do the same thing with your organizational values. However, the majority of the work should already be behind you, and this should be a shorter and easier process.

Organizational Values

What are the must-have principles that determine the direction and decisions of your organization? I can't overstate the benefits of setting these out thoughtfully with the process below.

All too often, I have seen a company's values splashed across on a web page and a few posters, but completely disregarded when it came to how the organization operated. That's when values work becomes a sad, though well-intentioned, waste of time and effort.

Fortunately, I have also seen organizations that constantly discuss their values and hold their choices up to the lens of the values. An organizational client of mine recently lit a fire under themselves and got serious about their values. They had had a major conflict with another company, and though my client came out on top, they had regrets about how aggressive and I-win-you-lose they had been. They wished instead they had worked for a win-win. When they did their values work, they affirmed that while they believe in being competitive, they will always prioritize a mutual win if possible. This is a great example of setting out a value that truly matters and drives behavior.

Here are two steps you can take to help you identify meaningful organizational values.

Step 1: Choose values that relate to performance

Allow me to state the obvious: Work is different from life. For one thing, it's about a product or service that must be successfully delivered, which means it's about performance. Your whole life is not as centered on performance, or at least it shouldn't be. For example, a key personal value might be about the love you express to your family. That love is an end in and of itself. But if love is part of an organizational value, you must tie it to how the company ultimately functions. For example, "We love each other, knowing that great relationships help produce great results."

That does not necessarily mean that every value you have must have a specific performance outcome attached to it. However, it does means that every value must *contribute to performance*. Here are some examples:

- Healthy culture
- Team-directed
- Excellence in results
- Deeply interested in the welfare of those who are hurting
- Integrity in all things
- Research-driven
- Market leader
- Driven to see kids reach their potential
- High customer satisfaction

You will be pleasantly surprised at how many values add up to a well-functioning organization. Successful companies don't succeed simply by working hard. It is never that simple. So give yourself a little time to think about the different divisions, teams, and people in your group, and who is doing what that makes a contribution. Then create values from that. For example, making a connection between the bonding your team experienced on a weekend off-site and the next quarter's outstanding results could lead you to a value of "trust is key to our performance."

Step 2: Identify the aspirational and observable values for your organization

Follow the same process for your organizational values as you did for your personal values. Write down what you want your organization or group to aspire to, and the observable values—healthy and unhealthy— you and your people are living out right now. One company I worked with discovered that their observable value was "employees have great relational connections, regardless of performance." The CEO was a bit aghast at discovering that, and quickly began working on "employees having great relational connections *and* great performance."

You will probably end up with considerably more than seven values at this step, and that's okay. In fact, the more the better. I've often found that the last few values are the ones that end up making the final cut. Perhaps because the longer you work the process, especially with others, the sharper your thinking becomes because your brain is learning how to do it over time.

Step 3: Pare down your organizational list by reviewing it in light of your personal list

This is simple. If any organizational value conflicts with your personal values, eliminate it. If it fits, it stays until you pare down your list to the top three to seven values. Most of the time, you will find that your organizational values fit. I can't think of an organizational value that a client wrote down, especially after working through personal values, that didn't fit somewhere.

Review these values, talk to others about them, and allow time to pass between reviews. Your brain works better when it has time to chew on material between concentration sessions. But when you find yourself doing nothing but polishing things up, it's time to bring them out to your organization. Working through them organizationally can include many initiatives:

- Asking staff for input, improvement, and buy-in.
- Presenting the final version at a formal staff meeting to show that this has gravitas.

- Having different people at each team meeting discuss what one of the values means to them and how it impacts their department or group.
- Creating visual reminders, such as web banners and posters, to keep the main thing the main thing.

A Values Example

Just as I do try to eat my own cooking, I wanted to share my personal and organizational values lists. After following the same process I just described, here is where my values landed.

Personal Values

Love (for God and people). I want to be connected in vulnerable relationships with God, my family members, and friends who matter most.

Responsibility. I will take ownership over my life and how I will spend my limited time and energy.

Living in freedom. I want to make free choices that are based on my values, not choices motivated by guilt, shame, or codependence.

Holiness. I will separate myself from the things that would keep me away from God and the path he sets for me.

Engagement in growth. I will involve myself with people and structures that promote my spiritual, personal, emotional, and relational development.

Meaningful career. I will invest my talents in work that advances my own mission in life, and provides for me and my family.

Service and giving back. I will be generous to those who are in need by sharing my finances, time, attention, and other resources.

Organizational Values

Mission alignment. Everyone understands and is committed to the part they play in supporting and advancing the mission of the organization.

Healthy culture. Our people engage in relationships, attitudes, and behaviors (RAB) that are professionally vulnerable, honest, and supportive.

High performance. We deliver great products and services and have metrics to ensure our accountability.

Continuous growth. We promote continuous growth for our people and our processes so we can stay current and achieve excellence.

Notice that there isn't a one-to-one correspondence between my personal and organizational values, but that there is a supportive relationship between them. For example:

- The organizational value of mission alignment relates to the personal value of a meaningful career. A large part of our time and effort on the earth is to accomplish something worthwhile that makes life better. In that way, we contribute to the biblical mandate to "fill the earth and subdue it" (Genesis 1:28). That is what a meaningful career does for us. And when the mission of the leader's organization ties into that, one's efforts are consistent and make sense.

- The organizational value of a healthy culture relates to the personal value of love. Culture, as I define it, is *how relationships, attitudes, and behaviors drive performance.* That is, the many ways we connect with, or actually love, one another in the workplace have a direct impact on how the company works. Love motivates, encourages, and energizes us. It is the actual "fuel" of our activities.

- The organizational value of high performance relates to the personal value of responsibility. We are to "own" our responsibilities in life and engage intentionally in following through on them. Taking care of our families and friends, being financially prudent, having good self-care, and having meaningful goals are all part of being responsible. This is the "doing" part of life. And the end game of an organization is to "do" or execute responsibly whatever is most important.

A friend of mine who owns a social media business said recently, "There is a big difference between getting a hundred thousand Facebook followers and meeting a pro forma goal for a client. If I am not responsible for the end result, I'll get fired— and I should. My actions must result in the performance the client needs." I could not agree more.

- The organizational value of continuous growth relates to the personal value of engagement in growth. Every leader has heard the phrase *continuous learning*. It refers to the need for a company to "grow or die." There is such a strong parallel between this organizational reality and what happens in our personal lives. Especially in brain growth and health, we know that people who live right, are curious, and actively challenge their minds are more likely to have well-working brains for many years.

As long as you can make a meaningful connection between your organizational values and your personal values, you are on the right path. By the way, I review these annually. Things change, and so do our priorities.

Remember that just as you are a living person, your organization has life as well. The organization is also an organism with a goal, direction, motivation, strengths, and weaknesses. The clearer you are on your personal values, the more you will help the organization to live into its values as well.

It All Comes Down to This

As a consultant coach, the best report card I get for my work is what the people around my clients—colleagues, direct reports, family—say about them after we've completed our work together. These are the ones who experience the impact of my clients' growth, or lack of it. One of my favorite report cards came from the board, direct reports, and wife of a CEO I coached. Their statements were especially meaningful to me:

- "He is bringing in great results," said a board member.
- "He is truthful and direct, but we also know he is on our side," said a direct report.
- "He is vulnerable and accessible emotionally," said his wife.

Each statement represents a positive change or growth in the CEO's life and leadership, and each is directly related to the values that he identified and then worked on in his life and job.

Ultimately, those who lead from their gut return again and again to their personal values as the foundation for their leadership objectives. That is why it is so worth it to make time on your calendar to do your values work. Landing your values and living them out will not only help you for the rest of your career, but for the rest of your life.

PART II

THOUGHTS

LEADERS THINK ABOUT THINKING

A longtime friend of mine, Jim, is a leader in the media industry. He is well respected for his insights, ethics, and the results he creates. I have had many conversations with Jim and have benefited from our friendship. There is a pattern I have noticed with Jim and other effective leaders that goes like this. You present some knotty problem to him—for example, one with complexities in finances, people's personalities, market economies, and so on. You describe the situation to him from all the angles you can. You tell him where you're landing on it. You tell him what other people have said so far. And you say, "So what do you think? Do I fish or cut bait on this situation?"

Having listened carefully and having asked several good questions, Jim will be silent for a moment. Then he will say, "Let me get back to you."

It can be frustrating at the time. You've spent all this energy dissecting the situation, and now you have to wait. But having gone through this experience many times with Jim, I have found that the wait is worth it. He will call me in a few days and give me some perspective I hadn't thought of, and it will generally be very helpful.

Here is the point: Not only had I not thought of the new perspective, but *neither had Jim, at the time.*

When I first presented the situation to him, he really didn't know what he thought yet. Jim wasn't putting me off as some sort of lesson in learning patience. He really hadn't yet formulated his final opinion. He was actively listening and learning. Certainly he had ideas and options running around in his head when I told him my situation. Most of us do. But he knew that was not the right time for him to think. He wanted to take in everything he could and then spend some time ruminating on it all.

This approach works well. This doesn't mean, of course, that friends and advisers who give you answers on the spot can't provide great wisdom. Certainly they can and do. But the Jims of the world have a high batting average. They *think*, and they respect the time it takes to think well and in a thorough manner.

Not only that, but the people whom Jim leads often feel the same way I do. The fact that he takes the time to think through their words and problems makes his answers significant and weighty to them. Those he leads and influences find this a major reason they follow him.

Believe it or not, there is a great deal of research devoted to the process of "thinking about thinking," which is called *metacognition*.[1] Researchers study how human beings think in order to help us improve our thinking process. In the same way, leaders who are intentional about "getting outside" themselves—by making it a habit to observe how they think—will find that they increasingly think more effectively and clearly.

It's common to characterize people as "thinkers" or "feelers." Thinkers are known for their logical and data-driven take on the world. Feelers are likely to be seen as emotionally and relationally intelligent. Although these characterizations can certainly be true and helpful in some ways, identifying yourself as exclusively one or the other isn't an asset when it comes to leadership. In fact, it's actually a deficit. Neurologically, human beings are not designed to be thinkers *or* feelers, but thinkers *and* feelers. While everyone has a preference and tends to lean more toward one or the other, leaders who identify themselves and behave as either thinkers or feelers aren't operating at their full capacity.

The reality is that *your heart has a brain, and your mind has a gut.* Whatever your preference may be, you don't have the option to ignore the other one, or—and this is a leadership disease—to delegate it to someone else. The best leaders *integrate* their thinking: they develop and rely on both their heart and their mind. And that is what the following chapters are designed to help you do.

Chapter 4

YOUR HEART HAS A BRAIN

Good leaders place a high value on thinking clearly and well. Most spend a great deal of time thinking, in all sorts of contexts. Sometimes it is alone in a room, reflecting. Sometimes it is in a decision-making meeting with colleagues. Sometimes it is an instant, under-the-gun process. But thinking is critical.

Thinking is an internal activity. When you consider whether or not one of your direct reports is in the right place for her talents, you are thinking. When you shift resources to a different area in the marketplace, that is thinking as well. When you consider what study materials to use with your small group in the next quarter, that is thinking. Just as with your values, your thoughts are part of what it takes to be a leader who looks inside and finds many things that are needed in order to achieve the best results.

As I mentioned earlier, thinking—the reasoning part of your life and leadership—is critical and central to your work. That is why leading with intuition also includes reason. You learn about your mind by using your mind. The apparatus you are working with is also what you are observing. The apparatus you are observing is also the apparatus you are observing it with! I say this not as a matter of trivia but because I want you to be aware that your thoughts aren't always the right thoughts because your mind is fallible. I see too many leaders who never question their thoughts or their mental tendencies and quirks, and their leadership suffers. So be aware that your mind can make mistakes—not just in the decisions it makes but in the way it actually makes those decisions. The more you know about your thinking patterns, the better equipped you are to lead well.

Thinking 101

As a leader, it's important for you to understand the basics of how you think. The simplest definition of *thought* is an idea in the mind. In other words, a thought is some solution, brainstorm, strategy, insight, or observation. It can be about anything, but in the context of leadership, we're generally referring to thoughts about people, opportunities, and problems, which are the things you need to concentrate on.

A helpful way to look at thoughts is to contrast them with reactions. When you *react* to a situation, you don't act freely and independently. It's more of a knee-jerk response. You make decisions based on internal factors ranging from fear, emotional impulse, and passion to old habits or people's opinions. While positive reactions can be fun (a quick joke in a meeting that eases tension), negative reactions can be detrimental to your leadership and can shortchange your impact. In contrast to reactions, *thoughts* look at alternatives, weigh consequences, consider costs and benefits, and exercise judgment. Certainly thinking can be taken to the extreme—the "paralysis of analysis"—but in the main, those who think thoroughly tend to make better decisions and tend to treat people in a way that makes people want to follow them.

I once consulted with the CEO of a service organization who, in many respects, was a brilliant man. He had an incredible memory and understood financial complexities very well. However, he tended to have the same answer for every significant problem, and it was the old engineer's solution: *If it doesn't work, use a hammer. If that doesn't work, use a bigger hammer.*

For this CEO, the hammers were always the same: tighten down on expenses and work harder. There was nothing wrong with that, but it didn't solve all the major problems the company had. They needed new and different ideas. They needed *thoughts*. But his ideas were basically patterned reactions to what had always worked for him in the past. Eventually, he and the company had to part ways because he was not providing the new thinking that would have helped both him and the company. The sad thing is, he could have had new thoughts since he certainly had the capacity. But I don't think he was very interested in or curious about his own "think," how he actually mentally came to his own conclusions.

You need to be intentional about keeping your mind in shape. There is a growing body of research that indicates we "use it or lose it" as we age. This is especially true with things like memory, vocabulary, and mathematics. Even if you don't retain all your mental abilities, you may be able to keep sharper during the time you exercise your brain. For example, several times a week, I try to work out with an electronic game gadget designed to improve mental functioning. My sons give me a hard time about not playing more fun games with the gadget, but it's no game to me. I want as much mind as I can have for as long as I can have it.

Five Practices of Successful Thinkers

There are several dimensions to how successful leaders think that are important to know, but I want to focus on five especially. If you want to develop your thinking, the following practices will serve you well.

1. Know Your Cognitive Style
Your cognitive style refers to the way you process information from your environment. It has to do with how you read journal articles, how you listen to what others tell you, and how you draw conclusions based on how you observe the workplace. One key aspect of cognitive style is whether your thinking tends to be *linear* or *nonlinear*.

Linear thinkers are more logical and ordered in how they think, while nonlinears come at problems and opportunities from different angles. Linear thinkers typically have a step-by-step approach to their work. Nonlinears try to see if there is a new way to look at an issue. This description is a broad one. People who research these matters disagree on what specific terms and descriptions to use, but for the purposes of this book, these distinctions describe the difference.

Linear and nonlinear cognitive styles tend to have stereotypes associated with them. Managers and accountants are often seen as linear. Their tasks involve numbers, finances, budgets, schedules, quotas, and planning. Marketing and public relations types tend to be seen as non-linear, with new ideas, promotions, analyzing the competition, keeping the attention of the consumer, and so forth. There certainly seems to be some basis in reality to these stereotypes. However, there are two problems people commonly encounter in stereotyping someone based on cognitive style. First, they tend to pigeonhole individuals into one style, and that can limit potential. Certainly, we have our dominant cognitive style that we need to work from. But most people aren't totally one or the other. You can utilize both.

For example, I know a woman who directs a small business in the communications industry, a sector in which there have been lots of changes over the years. She has had to wear many different hats in the company because of its size. The business wasn't large enough to hire full-time people for every type of role, so she had to learn to do some of the work herself.

Her background was as a vice president in the larger corporate world, where she ran a division and established policies that were essentially linear tasks. In the new position, however, she found that she needed someone to write marketing copy that was interesting and presented the new company's products well—nonlinear type of work. She decided to be that someone, so she sat down and began thinking like a marketing person. She wrote ads, product descriptions, and promotional e-mails. The market responded, and sales increased. She was surprised to find out that she enjoyed the work. She would still say that she is basically a linear thinker; however, she has not restricted her work to linear tasks. In fact, she now takes creative-writing courses and writes short stories as a hobby.

This happens in the other direction as well. An artist finds he has a knack for finance. A visionary is able to work with others on the steps required for that vision. A marketer can plot step-by-step strategies. The point is, while you have a primary cognitive style, don't limit yourself.

The second problem with stereotyping based on cognitive styles is the tendency to value one style over the other. This happens often in business and leadership circles. So the out-of-the-box thinker, who can think in terms of complexities and systems, is perceived as being more helpful to the organization than the linear thinker, who is seen as limited by A + B = C logic. On the other hand, the nonlinear thinker is criticized as irrational and unrealistic, even presumptuous, while the linear thinker is praised for attributes such as diligence and responsibility.

Either way, there is a danger to this sort of view. Stereotypes ignore the way leadership and organizations work. You need people with both cognitive styles. At different times in the company, the church, the family, or the small group, you may need to rely on one style over the other, for that particular season. But both cognitive styles are necessary in the long term. New ideas need a sound basis in reality and vice versa.

So in terms of your own cognitive style, you most likely know which basic way your mind tends to work. The best way to be intentional about keeping your mind in shape in this regard is to continue honing your dominant cognitive style while appreciating and cultivating the other style as well.

This is important for your leadership because you need to harness and develop both cognitive styles as you lead the people around you. People need to follow someone who can help them with logical progression and also with creativity as their own situations and styles mesh with yours.

2. Think Relationally

Being a clear and productive thinker requires the ability to craft thoughts and ideas in terms of relationships. Your mind didn't develop in a vacuum, apart from people. And it is a mistake to keep your thinking divorced from people—what they mean to you and how your thoughts will affect them. No matter what your area of leadership is, people are part of it. You lead people, you influence people, and you matter to people. Your organization has something to do with some service to people, whether a computer, a bank loan, a home, education, medical care, groceries, personal growth, or a retail outlet. This means it's necessary to keep people in mind when you create opportunities and solve problems. You can do this in two ways: connecting your thoughts, and considering the impact of your thoughts. Let's take a look at these two aspects of thinking relationally.

Connect your thoughts. Connecting your thoughts simply means bringing what you're thinking about to others. We are primarily designed to be relational beings, and real meaning and purpose derives from relationship. So the ideas, solutions, dilemmas, new visions, and improvements you come up with will do better when you talk about them with others. You engage with people, and they are drawn to what you are thinking. They are energized by and drawn to your leadership. You, in turn, are enriched by their contributions.

This is why I love spending time with people who love what they do and think about what they do, especially if it's an industry I know nothing about. I enter a world, guided by an expert with many years of experience, that is not only interesting to me but is usually quite valuable in my own work. Not long ago, I had a long talk with a neighbor who sells rockets. I had no idea what was involved. He told me about the design issues, how spacecraft is marketed, the process of selling and negotiation, and how he leads his sales team in a very long track, taking years per sale. Later, as I thought about what he had told me, I was able to better look at the long-term perspective in my own work and company, which didn't compare with the perspective he has to have in his industry.

This isn't to say that you shouldn't think at your desk, on a run in the hills, or while in a retreat setting. Thoughts that come in solitude can be very valuable. Whether you originate your ideas alone or in a meeting, make sure that on a regular basis someone, somewhere, knows what you are thinking. You aren't doing yourself or your spouse any favors when you get home, are asked how the day went, and respond with nothing more than "Fine." Get the ideas out; noodle them with your spouse or a close friend. If you do this regularly, you will not only think better but also become more connected to the important people in your life.

Consider the impact of your thoughts. The other part of thinking relationally is considering the impact of your thoughts. Whatever group you are leading, it matters ultimately to people because people are what matter. You affect the end users of whatever you are producing. You matter to those end users. Keep those end users in mind at all times. They have difficult and complex lives. You want to provide something that makes those lives better in some way.

Even if you enjoy pure thought, you need to consider your impact on people because you matter to them. A friend of mine is extremely talented in mathematics. He could teach it on a university level. He is in business, however, and has led several successful companies by capitalizing on his math abilities, especially as applied to the financial world. A few years ago, he left a very good position for another one that, while also a success, wasn't at the intellectually stratospheric level of the first one. His reason for the job change? He wanted a more direct connection to the end user, more access to people, and more hands-on experiences. He sees both jobs as having equal value; it's not a case of better or worse. For him, it is a matter of wanting to see faces, eyes, and hands using a product he has created.

This is what I mean by considering the impact of your thoughts. You will have an impact, one way or another. So keep your thoughts connected to relationships, and keep people's faces in front of you. There is no better way to have your thoughts integrated with the rest of your inner world than to be a relational thinker. We'll consider your relational world in greater depth in chapters 8 and 9.

3. Orient Yourself to Reality—with a Nod to the Positive
Another aspect of successful thinking is your orientation to reality. To be an effective leader, you need to think about what *is* going on, not what you would *like* to be going on. Reality happens, and it always wins. You must take the bad news with the good news, even if it reflects poorly on you. This is the only way you will ever make transformational changes in yourself and in the people you work with.

In the church I attend, the leadership made a commitment several years ago to allocate a high percentage of funds to a children's ministry building. Their reasoning was that while there were other worthy places to put money, the church is located in the middle of a growing community with lots of young families. They wanted to attract parents to come via the services the church had for the kids. These are leaders who are also committed to overseas work and fighting local poverty. They have high values connected to those needs, and it was hard to shift the finances during this time to a building. So it wasn't a reality they especially wanted to be true; it simply was what they believed to be true.

The leadership took a lot of criticism for this decision. People thought the money shouldn't go to brick and mortar but to direct services. The leaders listened to the complaints, but in time they went ahead with their decision. They were convinced of the reality that they could reach people in the best way by helping families get help. It was not a popular reality, but it was one they had researched and based their decisions on it.

Recently, a family with young children moved into our neighborhood. My wife and I invited them to church, and they went with us. While the grown-ups seemed to have a generally positive experience, it was the ten-year-old daughter who got their attention. When she returned from the children's ministry time, she told her parents she wanted to come back. Bear in mind here that she had moved to her new home from hundreds of miles away just two days before attending the church. She did not know a single soul there, but the warmth and quality of the program captured her heart. And many people in the community are now bringing their children for the same reasons.

The leaders thought in terms of reality, and they won in my book. They looked at what was, not what they wanted things to be. In your own leadership, face reality first. Get the bad news first. Really listen to the financial problems, personnel issues, and sales dilemmas. Good leaders think about reality first and then find solutions and opportunities second.

At the same time, I believe the thoughts of a leader should ultimately go toward the positive. No one is completely balanced between good news and bad news. So veer toward hope. That is what a leader's thoughts bring to those who are watching and depending on her. The people you lead need someone who can bear the bad, contain it, understand the depth of it, and still provide a realistic hope if one exists. Certainly, if it's time to roll up the show, that is the reality. But a good leader brings thoughts to the table that look at every scenario that can provide something good for people.

I have cohosted a daily call-in counseling radio show for many years, called *New Life Live!*[1] I have listened to thousands of callers present their struggles with troubled relationships, emotional issues, addictions, and the like. You face a lot of reality when you listen to people's personal problems. I often receive calls from individuals who have severe and complex problems, problems that certainly cannot be resolved in a few minutes on the phone. So I give them insights and perspectives for now, and then suggestions, steps, and resources for later, when the call is over. With the most hopeless-sounding situations, I have always tried to give something people could take away, something that was real and true and substantive, but also something that provided an option that they didn't have before they called. I don't know most of the endings of the stories. But I do know that all of us who desire to lead need to be mindful of the responsibility to have thoughts that are not only grounded in reality but also give hope at the end.

4. Be Willing to Hold Opposing Thoughts
Another mark of leaders who think well and successfully is that they are able to live in conceptual tension. They can listen to, and think about, ideas that are diametrically opposed. They have enough space in their minds to consider and analyze both sides while they are moving toward a decision.

This is not an easy task. We all have a tendency, as leaders, to think, *Plan A is better than plan B for these reasons, so let's go for A.* Because of the pressure and speed of leadership today, we simplify things to that level and move on. It becomes a zero-sum game: A wins and B loses. While that is often the right way to go, it is not always. Thinking leaders must resist the impulse to immediately discard an idea that is antithetical to one they like. If they can live with the tension for a while, they are apt to come up with even better solutions.

I have a good friend who is a great example of this. He is a consultant for companies that are ready to go to the next level of growth. On a recent consulting project, he was interviewing vice presidents of different departments, as is his habit, to get an overall feel for the nature of the company. What he found was a large division between marketing and accounting. This is a typical tension: marketing wants enthusiastic support for their energy and ideas, and accounting wants to cut unwarranted expenditures. But this company was more divided than usual. The two departments had locked horns, and their adversarial relationship was actually the problem keeping the company from going to the next level.

Marketing was convinced that the company was headed for a smaller market share, and ultimately disaster, if the company didn't make a big commitment to an aggressive ad campaign. Accounting saw no way that could work because the money was not there. The company was stretched thin as it was. There had been shouting matches and everyone calling on the CEO to take a stand on one side or the other. For his part, the CEO was torn, as he didn't know which answer was the right one. As the company's leader, he didn't want to alienate half the team by a decision, though he knew that might be the only answer.

My friend the consultant coached the CEO in this way: "You may have to take sides on this. But I don't think you have to yet. Begin with the premise that both perspectives have a lot of merit, and see if there is some way you can go in both their directions." In other words, it might not be a zero-sum game. The CEO agreed to take some time to think about the issue. That was the beginning of the turning point for the company.

With this new idea of holding opposing thoughts at the same time, the CEO finally landed on a solution. It involved some infusion of capital, large enough that marketing could do some trimming and still mount a major campaign, but small enough to satisfy accounting in case it backfired. The project worked, and the company did make it to the next level.

This doesn't mean you have to be open to absurdities. Some things just don't make sense. But it does mean that you have to at least consider two perspectives or opinions that don't agree. Don't immediately react and toss one out. Give your mind a little time to see if there is a win-win.

5. Adapt to New Realities and Truths

Related to holding opposing thoughts in tension is the ability to change and adapt when the facts dictate it. The best leaders know that reality is larger than they are, so they don't mind taking a different course when there is new information. Clear thinking means submitting your mind to any new reality.

I was working in my office and needed to use a piece of computer equipment I'd left at home. I called one of my teenage sons and, knowing he was busy with school activities, offered him ten dollars to stop what he was doing and bring me the equipment. Since it was a thirty-minute round-trip drive, it sounded reasonable to me. He said, "I'll do it for fifteen dollars." I didn't mind that response. I didn't play the guilt card or the "you owe your dad" card because I have talked to my sons a lot about money, time, and negotiation. I just said thanks but no thanks and hung up. Then I called his brother and left him a voice mail with the same request. I had a backup, having two sons who can drive.

About a minute later, the first son called me back and said, "I'll do it for ten dollars."

"Great," I said. "Why the change of heart?"

"When I hung up, I asked Mom if you were trying to teach me a lesson on negotiation," he said. "Mom said, 'No, he's going to call your brother.'" My wife understood the situation clearly. And my son quickly adapted to the new information and made the necessary changes.

Leaders who think will need the ability to admit when they are wrong or should change direction. Those who insist that the original plan is the only plan are often at risk. You instill doubt in people with that stance, and you instill trust in people when you adapt to new realities.

Let's wrap up this section with a tip I provide for many leaders I work with: *Make a habit of challenging your own logic.* That is, whenever you work through some problem and come to a decision point, vet and scrutinize your thinking process to see if it can stand up to scrutiny. Don't assume because you have done the due diligence of mapping out an answer to a problem that your thinker is infallible.

Let's say that you have just come up with a strategy to address the growth of a competitive organization. You looked at what they did, how they did what they did, brainstormed tactics that might help you compete better, thought through them, then picked one.

Great. Now do it again, and then bring it to a couple of truth-based associates and have them ask you the hard questions about how you arrived at your decision. If your thinking process was clear and effective, it will come out as a win. If not, you have just saved yourself from an expensive mistake, or what author Dave Ramsey calls the "stupid tax."

Too many leaders are too tired or bored or entitled to question their logic, and the outcomes are not good. Challenging your decision-making logic is a healthy sowing that will enable you to reap success in your organization. As the Bible teaches, "You will always harvest what you plant" (Galatians 6:7 NLT). This principle will never fail you.

Chapter 5

YOUR MIND HAS A GUT

Let's return to a statement from the assessment at the beginning of this book: *I have ignored my gut in making decisions and later realized it was a mistake.* I have discussed this issue with many leaders over the years, and almost all of them admit they have had this experience. You have most likely had it as well. It generally goes something like this: You interview an individual to fill a position. The person looks great on paper; the résumé and recommendations are fine. He or she interviews well and seems to fit the bill. Yet you have some weird sense that something isn't right about the person. You can't put your finger on it, but there is a negative response. However, with no rational reason to support that sense, you go ahead with the hire.

And then, within a few months, you find out what the weird negative response was about. It might be that the person has a poor work ethic; it might be a personality style that clashes with key people; sometimes it is a character issue or a moral problem. You can sense your gut tightening and chiding; your gut says to you, in so many words, *I told you so. Why didn't you listen to me?*

This sensation, often called *intuition,* is well known in leadership. However, it shows up in virtually every aspect of life, such as buying a home, choosing whether or not to ask someone on a date, or discerning if your child is lying about where she's been. But its existence poses a problem: How does the leader reconcile the two sorts of information—external and internal? What do you do with a sense or a response that doesn't seem to have a basis in facts? How can you best use the internal sources of your life to lead well and successfully? For starters, it helps to understand something about how intuition functions neurologically.

Intuition and Your Brain

As we discussed in chapter 1, the experience of intuition is drawing a conclusion about a person or a situation with no known basis for that conclusion.[1] An intuitive response is generally understood to be immediate, quick, and direct: *Stop. Go. Yes. No. Do it. Don't do it.* But, as you'll see, I believe this isn't merely an instinctual snap judgment. It may be quick, but there is a lot more than speed going on that leads to that intuitive decision.

There are many theories about what intuition is: an emotional reaction, a conviction of some reality with an as-yet-undiscovered source for it, a mystic experience, the voice of God. However, a good deal of research now indicates that rather than being a mystical and unknowable process, intuition may be a combination of two elements related to how we think and how we assimilate information. The first has to do with the analytical and logical aspects of the mind. This is the part of your brain that is linear and quantitative in nature. This part seems to have the capacity to think extremely rapidly and come up with conclusions almost instantly. It's as if, in computer language, the processor speed is almost incalculable. This aspect of intuition is logical yet very rapid. For example, a radiologist can look at an X-ray and almost immediately conclude what is wrong with a person's spine. She has looked at thousands and thousands of X-rays. Her mind rapidly does the work because this is known territory. But if this same radiologist is looking at a stock report, without a lot of experience, she may deliberate for hours on what decision to make. This is how the more left-brain process works.

At the same time, intuition also works from the creative, more spontaneous aspects of the mind. This is that hunch for which you can find no logical, informational, or data-based reason. You just *know*, and you know that you know that you know. It is the classic hunch with no supporting evidence. This aspect of intuition seems to be simply another way of reaching conclusions that does not follow a linear path. The path is more emotional and experiential.

A married couple I know is a good example of both aspects of intuition—the analytical and the creative. As with many couples, he is more rational while she tends to be more intuitive. They work together in leadership in the same organization. He tells me that he will not interview anyone for a position or a proposal unless she is also in on the process. There have been so many instances in which she would say, "He's going to be a problem," or "Don't let her get away," and she would have a very high hit rate. She would not be able to articulate the reasons, but she had strong senses of yes or no. The husband, seeing the same interviewee, may see nothing of what she experienced. But he has learned to trust her "knowing without knowing."

Intuition does seem to evidence itself more readily in areas in which you are competent and experienced. That is, when you know your subject well, your mind has many experiences, memories, patterns, and conclusions from which to draw. This experience base feeds the accuracy of the hunch.

Whether it originates from the more rational or the more creative aspects of the mind, intuition is a kind of thinking process, and any thought can be mistaken. You can have the wrong facts, or you can draw the wrong conclusions on the right facts.

For example, on a recent consulting project with a company, I came to the difficult conclusion that a thirty-year employee was at the center of many performance problems the organization was experiencing. He was not open to feedback, nor was he a team player. He had his own way of doing things and heaven help you if you crossed him. Unfortunately, his toxic behavior over the years had damaged the corporate culture. No one wanted to work with him, and when they did, things didn't go well.

Compounding these difficulties was the fact that the employee and the CEO had been very good friends since childhood, and the CEO had deep feelings of attachment and loyalty to the employee. So when I brought my observations to the CEO and made it clear that the employee probably had to go, the CEO didn't even let me finish my thoughts before he shook his head and snapped, "I don't even have to hear the rest of this, that's not an option. He's a valued asset." When I pressed a bit, the CEO simply dug in his heels and that was it. On the outside, he looked very confident and seemed sure that his quick judgment was the right course. I didn't know what was going on in the inside, but sadly, the outcome was that the company had to lose a great deal more in revenue and staff morale before he changed his mind. It was a situation well captured by the old saying, "Always confident and often wrong." Just because we *feel* that an intuitive response is the right move is no guarantee it actually is.

When I am consulting with leaders who believe it's best to always go with the gut every single time, I take them on a review of their past decisions. Sooner or later, we will find some instance in which intuition led them in a way that wasn't the best way. This includes even those, like the wife and business partner above, who have a very good track record.

The best way any leader can use her mind to think in ways that work for her organization is to remember that *reality is in charge.* It is not divided. There are no inner and outer realities that are ultimately opposed. Both sources of truth must be subject to what is truly true. So in an ideal setting, your intuition should agree with your conscious thinking.

When the two disagree, I believe there is generally something missing. Let's return to the earlier instance of hiring a person you felt weird about. Most likely, you didn't have enough information about that individual at the time. If you had dug deeper into the recommendations, or observed the candidate over a period of time in stressful situations, it's likely that the flaw—in either the candidate or your intuition—would have emerged. Then your intuition and the objective information would have worked together. That is why many businesses hire with a probationary period, so that time will tell the tale without a lot of damage in case things don't work out. Perhaps you're familiar with the Bible verse that says, "Do not be hasty in the laying on of hands" (1 Timothy 5:22). In other words, don't rush to put anyone into a leadership position. Significantly, this same principle also applies to the process of hiring staff. On the flip side, perhaps you felt great about a person who later proved to be a problem. In this case, there could be several reasons your intuition failed. You wanted that person's skill set so much you didn't pay attention to the warning signs. Or you tend to be overly optimistic and miss character flaws in others. Or perhaps you liked the candidate as a person but didn't check out his or her skill set deeply enough.

The real takeaway here is to think, observe, and learn from the experience. If intuition is a type of thinking, then anything that strengthens your conventional thinking will also hone your intuition. The more experience you have, the more able you are to observe patterns in people, and the more you are able to learn from your observations, the better fuel you have to grow your intuitive abilities. That is how intuition grows and develops for you. Don't put intuition on a pedestal, but don't ignore it either. A well-trained intuition is a good servant and a poor master.

Pay Attention to Your Thinking

So how can you become a wise, sober-minded person of good judgment—one who thinks rather than reacts and routinely utilizes internal as well as external data? You can start by becoming an observer of how you think. As I said, it may sound strange to think about thinking, but it is important and helpful. You can begin to pay attention to your thinking by routinely observing your thoughts and by recognizing any cognitive distortions.

Observe Your Thoughts—Without Trying to Control Them

Life is chaotic, and sometimes too much information can cause confusion in an organization. As a result, leaders are under great pressure to think with focus and direction. It is an important task.[2] Sometimes, however, leaders interpret a need for clarity as a need to control their thoughts and keep them directed and precise. This is a problem. Leaders need to provide clarity to their organizations, but they need to also observe where their thoughts are leading and what they mean. There is much value that can come from observing your thoughts.

For example, think about someone in your organization who, when you are engaged in a conversation with him for more than a minute or two, your thoughts begin to wander. It can be like the movie scenes where a bored high-school student enters some daydream while his teacher drones on, then startles back to reality when she stands over him, saying, "Do you understand my question?" When talking to this person at work, you find yourself thinking about golf, lunch, or your date that night. As a result, you miss what the other person is saying and have to quickly catch up somehow so he won't notice.

You may be tired. You may not be interested in the topic. But there are other reasons you may be thinking those particular imaginative thoughts. And if you understand those reasons, they can point to something valuable for you, the leader. For example:

- He rambles on about details no one cares about, and he needs to be coached to be succinct.
- He talks in an egocentric way about only his perceptions, and he needs to be helped to consider other people's experiences and viewpoints.
- You are annoyed with him about something, so you detach from him via your imagination. You may need to rectify that.
- He is bringing you negative news you don't want to hear. You may need to hear it anyway.
- You can't sufficiently detach from whatever you were doing and pay attention to him. You may need to refocus on him and return to the previous issue after the conversation.

Do you see all the potential these observations have to add value to your leadership? You can go beyond the symptom to the root cause and deal with it effectively. This is a far better use of your time and energy than not questioning your experience because, more often than not, the problem will only get worse over time.

The point is, you need to be willing to look at not only *what* you are thinking but *how* you are thinking. This process will pay off for you in the long term.

Recognize Cognitive Distortions

As part of observing your thoughts, you also need to be aware of ways your thoughts can be distorted or misleading. Psychologists refer to these biases as *cognitive distortions*, or patterns of thinking that aren't reality-based and therefore hinder your productivity.[3] There are several distortions that can hamper a leader's thinking. As you read through the list below, see if you recognize any of these patterns in your own thinking and decision making.

- *Helplessness*—the sense of "I've tried and nothing helps," as if there are no choices available to you.
- *Passivity*—a pattern in which you are afraid or hesitant to take initiative, so you wait for someone or some circumstance to provide the solution.
- *Negativity*—a well-known pattern in leaders in which there is an imbalance of negative over positive. It is often justified as being "realistic," but it is generally built on fear of failure, not reality.
- *Self-protective rationalizing*—a scenario in which you are unable to own your own contribution to a problem or to see another person's feedback as superior, so you rationalize your position to the point of uselessness.
- *One-solution thinking*—the idea that there is only one answer to a situation. This kind of thinking is very limited and is usually produced by anxiety or a perfectionist streak. For example, "We need more clients in our medical center, so let's advertise more." Who knows, maybe it's that plus community outreach plus better pricing plus warmer customer relationships. Sometimes there is only one answer, but most of the time there are several. The best thinking occurs when you look at various scenarios and play them out, either in your mind or with others.
- *False-self thinking*—when you try to be someone you're not by projecting an idealized or false version of yourself. You do this either to please people with that image or to keep yourself from seeing your own faults. It becomes a very restricted way of living and leading.

We all have some of these patterns to one degree or another. Identify the ones you might be challenged by. Then do a reality check with a couple of trusted and honest people who know you well. If the patterns exist, commit a thirty-day practice of reviewing the decisions you make each day. For each decision, look for any evidence of the cognitive distortion patterns you identified. Simply being aware of your patterns will go a long way in helping you to correct the problem. Once you are more aware, then ask a couple of well-grounded people, "How would you have thought about this issue?" Having others model healthy ways of thinking will help you to continue moving yourself in that direction.

Creativity and Leadership

What would you give to have been a fly on the wall at different great moments in leadership, especially those in which a creative idea changed the whole paradigm? For example:

- Henry Ford comes up with a mass-produced car.
- Fred Smith starts Federal Express, a faster and more reliable way to ship goods.
- Bill Gates begins Microsoft at age nineteen.
- Pierre Omidyar lands upon a new business concept that becomes eBay.
- Elon Musk founds Tesla, specializing in high-capacity electric cars.
- Jack Dorsey, Noah Glass, Biz Stone, and Evan Williams come up with an idea to make it easy to send "short bursts of inconsequential information" via SMS, called Twitter.
- Reed Hastings, CEO of Netflix, invests in video streaming, knowing he will destroy a successful DVD-by-mail service, but that it's the necessary foundation for long-term future success.

Through the ages, leaders have always been associated with innovation and creativity. Creative leaders are valued, and their contributions make a difference. Your thoughts have the potential to come up with creative ideas that can change and improve your organization, department, church, group, or family. Think about the last time someone in your organization came up to you and said, "We have a problem with X. What can we do?" Like most leaders, you probably felt the pressure that X is now your problem. You're the leader. You must come up with a solution that no one else has. It's in your lap. That is real pressure. But your creativity can go a long way toward coming up with a solution, a new take on things, or a new idea that can move your group forward.

Creativity is one of those attributes that tends to be misunderstood, so it's important to define it, especially in the context of leadership. Creativity is, simply put, the ability to rearrange existing components into a new whole. That is, you take what you see, organize it in a different way, and come up with a new idea, a new solution, a new service, a new structure, or a new product. Ford, Smith, Gates, Omidyar, and all the rest saw a need and an opportunity in business. Business was the context they were observing and thinking about. Sometimes it seems that creativity means coming up with something out of nothing. Think, for example, of an artist in a windowless room who paints a landscape masterpiece out of his head. However, that artist has memories and experiences to draw from. And that is what makes creativity so accessible: we all have the raw components for creativity lying around in our lives.

It used to be that creativity was viewed as an ability for only those who had a special gift. Either you were creative, or you weren't. While there certainly seem to be those individuals who are innately highly creative, it is now understood that everyone is creative at some level. And in today's rapidly changing world, that is an ability every leader needs to develop.

When it comes to creativity, the challenge leaders sometimes have is less with the value of creativity itself than it is with several myths that often surround it. See if you can relate to any of these myths about creativity in your own leadership context.

MYTH: Creativity Operates Best in Solitude
REALITY: Creativity Operates Well Collaboratively

Creativity thrives when you are in relationship. Great ideas come out of people supportively tossing ideas around in a team. Originally developed in 1994, the PlayStation gaming platform was developed by a team of more than one hundred people.[4] Over twenty years later, this product is still going strong and continues to be supported and developed by a large team. Solitude certainly plays a large part in the creative process since you need time away from distractions to think productively. But the more relational you are, the better input you can use from others, and the better feedback you receive for your own thinking.

MYTH: Creativity Requires a Blank Slate
REALITY: Creativity Requires Your Leadership Context

Creativity generally doesn't come out of a vacuum. It arises from opportunity and need. There is an environment, a context, a setting for the creative process. A creative leader learns to look at her situation and asks how this can be done better.

Several years ago, my friend and business associate Henry Cloud invited me and another psychologist named David Stoop to partner with him and psychiatrists Frank Minirth and Paul Meier in a medical and psychological treatment company that would provide both inpatient and outpatient care. Part of the inpatient program included a teaching element, in which we taught principles of emotional and relational growth and healing. Some of the topics concerned depression, anxiety, addictions, intimacy, trust, relationships, and the spiritual life.

We wanted to also make the insights we gained through the inpatient program available to people who weren't in a hospital setting but who wanted life to be better or to grow or heal in some area of life. We thought the information and approach could help people, no matter what their life settings. So we started thinking of ways to get the information out. We knew that in Southern California, where we are located, public seminars were popular in all sorts of areas: finances, health and fitness, cooking, relationships, and personal growth. So we rented a hotel ballroom and began speaking every Monday night on some topic of personal growth. One of us would lecture for an hour on a subject and then answer questions from the audience for another half hour. We called it Monday Night Solutions.

The talks seemed to meet a need, and enough people attended that we decided to continue it after a trial period. Ultimately, we conducted these talks for eighteen years, live, almost every week of the year. Next, we recorded the Monday Night Solutions talks in a studio and partnered with a media company to distribute them by satellite to a large number of subscribing churches in North America.[5]

People sometimes ask how we thought of a creative idea like a weekly live talk. My answer is that we simply *rearranged some existing components into a new whole.* Experts have been giving talks for a long time. The need was there, and the idea came. The creativity lesson for me in this area was not to try and come up with some creative idea out of the blue, but to focus on my leadership context—to see what was there and then see if it could be improved on.

Starting with your context will work for your own life and leadership as well. Here are some questions to help you think more creatively about improving your own situation. You can think through these questions on your own, or discuss them with a few people you are partnering with.

- What challenge is my organization facing today that isn't responding to simply working harder?
- If I had infinite resources at my disposal, how would I solve this challenge? Is there a way I can solve it in a similar way with the resources I do have?
- If this challenge is merely a symptom, what is the deeper need or issue in my organization that it might be pointing to? Is there a way to meet that need?
- What organizations outside my industry or context are solving challenges similar to mine in unorthodox or creative ways?

You will be surprised at how starting with an identified need or challenge can generate new ideas.

MYTH: Creativity Is a Chaotic Free-for-All
REALITY: Creativity Is Pro-Structure

There is a myth that the creative process can only be unleashed when you get away from all order, discipline, and parameters. People who believe this say that creativity must be as free as possible to express itself. This sort of thinking is not true, and it too often discourages leaders from investing in the process. Leaders know the value of structure in organizations. They aren't about to abolish all that in the hope that creativity might happen.

The reality is that creativity not only flourishes with structure, it often *requires* some sort of limit. Part of that structure includes limits on time, human resources, and finances. We aren't doing ourselves any favors by taking ten years to come up with a great business idea. My experience with people is that the idea is likely to come about at the end of year nine! As the saying goes, work expands to fill the time allotted to it.

Responding to limits is simply how the human brain works. It likes having *some* information and time, but it gets fatigued and overwhelmed with *infinite* information and time. It wants to make a good decision, feel okay about it, and go to the next thing! So limits are very helpful, not a hindrance.

A good friend of mine, Greg Brenneman, who was CEO of Continental Airlines, Burger King, and Quiznos, has a great habit. When he needs someone to make a presentation to a team, he requires that all the info be on one page. He told me that the responders get tired and distracted with too much information, and it isn't necessary for them to make the right decisions in the first place.

So don't hesitate to add structure and limits to your creativity repertoire and process. Overall, structure promotes rather than limits creativity.

MYTH: Creativity Arises from Misery and Unhappiness
REALITY: Creativity Is Pro-Health

The movie *Amadeus* vividly portrays Mozart's out-of-control life. Van Gogh's brilliance is often associated with his madness. But the "tortured artist" myth doesn't hold up in reality. Creativity is enhanced by personal and emotional health and the growth process in general. It flourishes in a fulfilled environment.

Think of your mind as having a certain amount of room in it, like the RAM of a computer. RAM is used for the "thinking" a computer has to perform. The more RAM, the better and faster the machine operates. When too many applications are open, however, there is less "operating" room, and the computer can become sluggish or inoperable. In a broad sense, the clearer your life and mind are, the more space creativity has to operate and grow in your leadership.

A childhood friend of mine, Dr. Larry Bell, is an accomplished composer. A Juilliard graduate, he is chair of music theory at the New England Conservatory of Music and associate professor of composition at the Berklee College of Music. I visited Larry at a class reunion some time ago, and during our talk, I asked him about the "tortured artist" theory. He said, "It hasn't been true in my experience. When I went through very unhappy times in life, I didn't compose as well. And when my life and relationships have been fulfilling, I have done my best work." Larry's life and productivity are evidence that creativity is pro-health. As noted psychoanalyst Dr. Karen Horney has stated, "An artist can create not because of his neurosis, but in spite of it."[6] I like to ask people who hold to the tortured artist idea, "What if Mozart and van Gogh had had good lives? What works might they have produced then?" And the same is true for you. Health and growth are good for you and for your creative development.

MYTH: Creativity Just "Happens"
REALITY: Creativity Requires Intentionality

There is an idea about how creativity happens that goes like this: *I was walking down the street and all of a sudden, the model for the next killer app came to me, and well, the rest is history.* We like this idea because it makes creativity exciting and spontaneous. And something like this has happened to me from time to time. But the norm for me, and for every successful creative person I know, is that such experiences are the exception.

Creativity, especially for the leader, takes work and discipline. You must allot time, room, and energy for creativity—both in developing it and in using it. I recommend that leaders read up on creativity, learn from experts, and get to know the process. There are many structured experiences and exercises designed by creativity experts to help you look at matters from a different angle and build your creativity muscles.

A client of mine who has a very successful enterprise in the agriculture industry is a great example of this. He began noticing that farmers and ranchers tended to give all the business power to distributors (those who package and resell the produce to chain grocery stores), mainly because the distributors had great systems and infrastructure that made that process easy. My client took some time off with me to simply think through his opinion that, ultimately, the producer (farmers and ranchers) had more intrinsic value than the distributors. As a result, he developed a provider-based negotiating strategy for dealing with his distributors, which simply had not been done before. And after a few months, he had significantly more control over that sector of his business than he had ever had—and more than other suppliers had as well. But it all started with him putting the time in to think about the issue from a new and creative perspective.

Use creativity intentionally. In your work relationships, tell people you need to think about things creatively. Have meetings dedicated to finding a new way to take advantage of an opportunity or to solve a knotty problem. Don't make the mistake of waiting for the inspiration to come. It can and it does, certainly. All of us have had an *aha!* experience of some kind. But that generally comes only after you have first been intentional in thinking creatively.

Using Your Gut to Think Leader Thoughts

As a leader, you simply must think differently. That includes not only applying your thinking to the traditional and expected tasks of leadership, but using your gut to think "leader thoughts." What I mean is that a leader's job is not only to connect with people, inspire them to greatness, and think strategically about the path to success, but also to think in ways that prove that he or she has earned the hat of leadership. This is the world of ideas. You have the hat because you are expected to have ideas that others don't have.

One of God's greatest gifts to you is your mind, your thinker. Take responsibility for all of its complex potential. In other words, take some risks and trust your gut. Ask yourself often, "Why am I thinking what I'm thinking in this situation right now?" Immerse yourself in the creative process and see things from a different slant, making leadership decisions based on that slant.

During any election season, we see a great deal of emphasis on which candidate has the best ideas. Certainly the candidates' personality, warmth, and maturity play a large part. But when it comes to voting for national political leaders, people want to see who has the best ideas about things such as the economy, national defense, taxes, health care, and a host of other areas. When a candidate presents a new solution, it makes headline news.

This doesn't mean that you, in your context, need to have all the best ideas. But you do need to create a setting in which the best ideas can arise. Sometimes that may mean bringing in someone who has the best ideas. Recruiting an expert is a good idea in itself. It is also what good leaders do.

You need to be ahead of the pack. You need to think farther ahead than those you lead, so you can look beyond what is going on now. Your thoughts, your leader thoughts, can move your organization or group to a new place of growth and achievement because you took the time to think like a leader.

Perhaps the best way to summarize all of these principles and skills about thinking is this: *Start experimenting with your thought life in new and different arenas.* You may be the most logical and rational leader in the world, but that doesn't mean you don't have anything left to learn about how to improve your thinking. Have some fun and take some risks.

Having presented the importance of understanding thinking—that your heart has a brain and your mind has a gut—we now move to an exciting but sometimes controversial area in leadership, which is the role and function of emotions. A central part of the inner life, your feelings can be a great asset to you and to your leadership.

PART III

EMOTIONS

THE UNLIKELY ALLIES IN LEADERSHIP

I was talking to Alan, an executive who was in charge of several departments. He was telling me that he struggled with an "attitude problem" in connection with one of his direct reports, a manager. "What kind of attitude problem?" I asked.

"Well, I get frustrated easily with him," he said. "Sometimes I even get angry with him, though I don't like to admit it. I don't think I'm being fair about this. I'm not that way with anyone else who reports to me, just him. I wish I could get over this attitude. I just need to stop being mad."

"That may be," I said. "But let's look first at what's going on. What do you get frustrated about with him?"

Alan said, "Well, actually, lots of things. He's a nice guy, and people like him. And he is valuable to the company. But he is so disorganized. I can't get information from him when I need it. He doesn't get his reports in on time. He's like a traffic jam in the company; everything slows down because of him."

"Then there may be good reason for your frustration," I said. "What have you done about it?"

"I've talked to him a million times, but his behavior doesn't change. So I have to spend more time managing this manager than I do everyone else combined." Then

Alan returned to his original thought. "But I don't like being angry like this. Show me some way to turn the anger around."

"Let me suggest something else," I said. "Maybe you *should* be frustrated and angry."

"Should be? But I'm not an angry type of guy."

"That's my point," I said. "You're no raving rage-aholic. You're a pretty even-keeled person, I know that. So maybe what's going on *should* be bothering you, and it's telling you to fix the problem."

"Fix it how?"

"Well," I said, "somehow you need to arrange things differently. There are several ways you might do this. You can find a way in which he gets his act together. Or you find someone who can manage him so you don't have to. Or you can find him another area to work in that doesn't require that he be organized. Or he may have to leave. But one way or another, I don't think the solution is to stop being angry. It's to *fix what is making you angry.*"

Alan thought about it and got it. He went to work on the situation. And in time, what worked was the second suggestion. Alan had the person report to someone else, who then reported to Alan. As a result, Alan's "attitude problem" went away. He wasn't frustrated and angry anymore. The new supervisor certainly had a challenge, but he had more time to allocate to the person than Alan did, so he wasn't as bothered. The individual did pretty well in the new situation and even became somewhat more structured because of the new arrangement.

Here is the point: your emotions can be your friend and your ally as a leader. When you lead from your gut, you seek out your emotions and utilize what they bring you. The chapters in this part explore ways to help you do just that.

Chapter 6

HARNESSING BOTH NEGATIVE

AND POSITIVE EMOTIONS

FOR LEADERSHIP

As a leader, how do you view your feelings? Do you enjoy them? Look forward to them? Discuss them frequently?

Probably not.

If you are like most people in leadership, you most likely view your emotions with some reserve. Leaders, to a large extent, have learned from experience that emotions are something to be controlled and mastered, and not much more than that. Emotions are rarely seen as accelerating leadership abilities.

In leadership circles, you tend to hear, "I'm interested in what you *think* about . . ." more than "I'm interested in how you *feel* about . . ." More value is attributed to the cognitive part of the inner world than to the emotional part. It is part of the leadership culture. That is why I was struck by Alex's comment about anxiety that I mentioned in the introduction to this book. Remember that Alex didn't pay attention to the uneasiness he felt in his gut about developing a product line that was outside the company's core business. He had the feeling, but he dismissed it. Feelings aren't always the magic key to a great leadership decision, but they *must not be ignored.*

Sometimes leaders describe a thought as a feeling (a typically male phenomenon). For example, the leader will say, "I feel that we need to allocate more resources to marketing." But that is not an accurate expression of emotion. Emotions aren't ideas; they are internal responses.

There are, of course, good reasons for hesitation when it comes to incorporating emotions in leadership. We have all seen situations in which a leader gave vent to some emotion and made a huge error in judgment. Or we've been in other situations in which fear and anxiety caused a leader to shrink back rather than boldly move forward, and bad outcomes followed. Or we've witnessed how intense feelings alienated a leader from those close to him. The leader who has constant emotional displays tends to create a negative impression of his competence.

I got a good reminder about the potential negative impact of emotions when I was recently called up for jury duty. I took a few days off work and listened to the arguments of the plaintiffs and the defense. At the end of the arguments, the judge ordered us to deliberate and come up with a verdict. As part of her instructions to us, she said, "You may have had emotional reactions to the people you have listened to. But don't let your emotions cloud your judgment." And she was right in saying that. Some of the jury members had a negative response to the style of one of the people in the trial. We had to keep refocusing ourselves on what the law said, what the truth was, and what the real issues were. It was the only way we could deliver a verdict that was just and fair.

Having acknowledged, then, that emotions can present a real problem in leadership, I want to present the other side and show that emotions not only can be helpful but are, in fact, essential to successful leadership. Remember what I wrote in the introduction about the dangers of *not* paying attention to emotions? *If you choose to ignore the soft data—your intuition—you do so at your peril.* That warning is probably most true in this arena of the emotional world.

A client of mine who was very successful in the tech investment world had made his mark during an upturn season. He had good instincts and was a risk taker by nature, so he functioned well in a boom market. However, when the market took a downturn and his associates began to make more conservative investments, he ignored the signs and continued his high-risk ways. That approach cost him a great deal. When I asked him about all this, he said, "I did feel anxious like everyone else, but I didn't pay attention to that. I just figured it was a sign of weakness." My client has since recovered from his losses, but he is now much more respectful of his emotions, especially his anxiety.

What are *emotions* or *feelings*? A good and simple working definition is that emotions are *subjective reactions*. Emotions include positive reactions, such as tenderness, happiness, or satisfaction. They also include negative reactions, such as anger, anxiety, or sadness. Emotions can be intense, or they can be subtle. They can be absolutely overwhelming, or we can be totally unaware that we are having them.

Like anything else inside you, emotions don't exist of and for themselves. Your emotions have a function, a purpose, a role. When you understand this role, you can harness your emotions to lead others well.

The Signal Function

Your feelings exist as a signal to you. They alert you that something is going on, something you need to pay attention to and deal with. That *something* may be an event outside of you or one inside. Look at your emotions as you would the instrument panel on a car. The panel includes gauges and indicators that provide information on things like fuel level, engine temperature, RPM, oil level, and tire pressure. When the indicators are in the proper range, you don't notice them because they signify that things are going normally. But when the indicators turn red, blink, beep, or light up, you pay attention because things are now not normal. The indicators are alerting you that something—usually a problem—needs to be taken care of.

In one of my first full-time jobs, I drove a company car about thirty miles with the oil light on. In my ignorance, I assumed it was like the gas gauge, and I figured I had a while before the oil was out. But by the time I barely made it back to the job site, the car needed major repairs. My boss was exceptionally kind to me despite my foolishness, but he did sit me down and explain what to do the next time the oil light went on.

That is what emotions do for you, and why it's good to understand what they mean and what to do about them. They point to a situation. Most of the time, there is some action you can take that will resolve the situation. The result is that the emotion gradually lessens in its intensity. Its job is done, so the emotion dissipates until the next time.

Take Alan's situation, described at the beginning of part 3. Alan wanted to stop having the emotions of anger and frustration. He didn't like feeling them, which is understandable. These are unpleasant emotions and no one wants to be angry all the time. However, his solution of simply trying to not be angry wasn't working. Using the car analogy, he was effectively trying to take a hammer to the oil light, smash it, and then say, "Okay, problem solved." But the real problem, the situation that caused the indicator light to blink in the first place, wasn't solved, and only got worse over time. When Alan instead decided to heed the warning light by distancing himself from the disorganized individual, his frustration and anger dissipated—not because Alan was trying very hard to not feel them but because he solved the real problem.

There are schools of thought that say that you can simply choose to feel, or not to feel, certain emotions. The theory is that feelings always follow our thoughts. So if you change your perspective, then your feelings will follow suit. Could Alan have learned more patience with his direct report and been less angry? He could have, in time. If he had had no other options available to him, he may have had to do that. Sometimes that does help us, as we grow, to become more mature and have a larger view on things. But that isn't always the best thing to do with our feelings. The best thing is to first look at the meaning of the emotion, see what causes it, and then deal with that.

Emotions aren't always a signal of something going on "out there," as was the case with Alan and his manager. They can also alert you to something you need to face within yourself as well. Sometimes an external circumstance will trigger a feeling, and sometimes an internal state of affairs will do the same. It's very important to a leader to know the difference.

For example, once when I was consulting with an executive team, I found myself feeling unreasonably irritated at one guy. When he talked, he annoyed me, and I felt like someone was scratching fingernails on a chalkboard. As I drove back to the hotel at the end of the day, I tried to figure out why he bothered me. What the man had said was fine, and he was a nice enough guy. Then it hit me: his voice and mannerisms reminded me of another guy I knew who truly was annoying and irritating! Once I made the connection, I felt more positive toward the man on the executive team. I realized then that I still needed to work on my feelings about the other guy.

Why is cultivating this kind of awareness important to a leader? Because your decisions must be based on as much clarity as possible. If you don't scrutinize your emotions, you are in danger of losing clarity, and that can damage how you lead your organization. You don't want to be opposed to someone because they remind you of a person from your past. Nor do you want to dismiss negative emotions toward someone out of concern that you're overreacting. You need to think through what's going on. (For additional guidance on how to do this, see "How to Read Your Emotional Signals" below.)

As signals, emotions can dispense positive or negative information. Either way, you need to pay attention to them.

How to Read Your Emotional Signals

- *Identify the feeling.* Are you anxious, frustrated, angry, sad, ashamed? The more specific you can be, the better equipped you'll be in knowing how to handle it.
- *Determine the external trigger.* Is it a conversation that didn't go well? Some bad financial news? An upcoming meeting you're dreading?
- *Consider whether or not there is an internal trigger.* Is the feeling more intense than it should be for the circumstances? Could you be reacting to some old thoughts, losses, or relational issues? If so, write them down and talk to a wise friend to help you connect the dots so you can separate the past from the present.
- *Make the best decision.* Great leadership is about making the best choices based on the data you have. Use both what you feel and what you think to make the best move.

When Alan walked through this process, he identified his feelings as frustration and anger. He knew the external trigger was his underperforming direct report. It was clear to me that he wasn't over-reacting, so it seemed unlikely that his frustration had an internal trigger (a disorganized person in his past who drove him crazy). If that had been the case, I would have had him tell me about that relationship, the negative impact on Alan and the organization, and how it made him feel. In most cases, just the fact that he understood the underlying issues would be enough to resolve the feelings. Alan had the clarity he needed to make the best move by rearranging the reporting structure.

Negative Emotions

As a leader, you really can't afford to ignore your negative emotions. In fact, they are critical to your success. I have to challenge many leaders about this because they are concerned that talking about anything negative will diminish their effectiveness. They would much rather be positive, energetic, and focused on taking the next hill. I'm as much a take-the-hill person as the next, but a team that doesn't learn from the defeat on the previous hill is in jeopardy of repeating that defeat.

Every competent leader will look at things like negative financial reports, market problems, and sales issues, and dig into them, as the saying goes, "eating problems for breakfast." The same needs to be true with negative feelings. They're just information, and they mean something. Don't minimize your negative emotions and say, "That's too much of a downer." Figure out what the data says, and you will be better off.

To help you do this, let's take a closer look at a few of the distressful or negative feelings we have and consider what they convey to us.

Anxiety: I Need to Protect Myself from a Potential Threat

Anxiety is a sense of unease, fear, or dread that signals you to move away from something or someone. It is a sign of danger or a lack of safety. Sometimes it is experienced in physical ways, such as a queasy stomach, sweaty palms, or a rapid heartbeat. Anxiety is a helpful emotion because it warns you that you may be in a situation that is not good for you. Many leaders have experiences in which they ignored their anxiety and made an error as a result. Other times, leaders misinterpret their anxiety, assuming a threat or a problem that doesn't really exist. Either way, anxiety is a signal to take self-protective action.

A friend of mine told me that he found himself dreading any interaction with his new boss. He avoided the man and tried to cut short any conversation. When I asked him why, he said, "He's really distant with me; he's not friendly. I don't think he likes me."

I knew his boss, and I didn't think he was that kind of a person. I also knew that he actually did like my friend; in fact, he had told me so.

"Is it possible that he's a little reserved?" I asked. "Maybe his seeming distance is not directed at you. I have always seen him as simply a little on the quiet side."

Thinking about it, my friend said, "It could be; I never thought about it."

My friend's previous supervisor had been a very gregarious and warm person, the kind of person who took initiative to really get to know others and was genuinely interested in them. In comparison, the new boss seemed cold and aloof.

"Why don't you make the first move and ask him how things are," I suggested. "Maybe he needs that."

That pretty much solved the problem. Despite his anxieties, my friend started taking the initiative with his boss. He would simply walk up to his boss and ask how the weekend had been or what his plans were for that night. The result was that the boss began warming up to him, and their relationship markedly improved. Certainly, it would have been better had the boss done the initiating himself, but that wasn't the situation. So in this case, the anxiety signaled that my friend was misinterpreting his boss's reserve as dislike. And when he took the action step, he solved the problem, which then resolved the anxiety.

There are other times, however, when anxiety signals a real-time, actual, and objective danger to be avoided. In these instances, instead of powering through, we need to stop, feel the feeling, understand the source, and take the right action steps.

For example, some time ago, I was approached by a man with a business offer. He wanted me to invest in a communications company that was starting up with a new concept. It seemed to be quite sound and a very good idea, with lots of upside. The only hitch was that he needed me to make a decision very quickly. As he said, "The ship is leaving the dock."

I needed more time to do due diligence and research the situation. At the same time, I hated missing what could be a great opportunity. So I tried to get as much information as I could in the little time I had. As I thought about the matter, I realized I was becoming anxious. I was feeling some fear about what was going on. At first, I thought I was just having the normal jitters before taking a risk. But it didn't go away. It got worse. In fact, the anxiety quickly became greater than my initial excitement about the opportunity. Finally, I figured out the nature of the anxiety: *I did not have sufficient time to get enough information to commit with confidence.* I wanted to say yes, but I could not. So I had to say no.

It turned out that my anxiety did me a favor, as the company didn't fare well. Anxiety says avoid this or go the other way, and I did. But again, the anxious feelings weren't the issue. They simply pointed to the reality I had to face, which was that I was being asked to rush to judgment. For many of us, the fact that someone doesn't give us a lot of time to decide is a warning sign that there is trouble. Maybe it should have been for me. Regardless, the experience demonstrates how helpful your anxiety can be, if you listen to it.

Anger: I Need to Deal with a Problem

Anger is a call to address conflict. When we need to face down an obstacle or right a wrong, our energy level rises and we prepare to confront or combat the situation in some way. Anger is a signal that there is a problem to be solved. It urges us to fix something that needs to be fixed. Again, anger can be a response to an external event or to an internal experience, but it must be addressed and dealt with. What makes us angry is not always a bad or difficult person, but at least a bad or difficult situation we want to see changed. We don't like to see people we care about getting hurt. Or diligently planned projects go south. Or our efforts to reach out to someone result in us being blamed or attacked. Such situations often provoke an angry response. This emotion can last a few seconds, or it can run for days and weeks. But the idea is that your anger is urging you to deal with a problem.

There are many war stories about the raging executive who yells, intimidates people, and slams his fist on the desk. He is certainly engaged in battle, but most of the time, his anger is not solving anything. People sometimes talk about how good it is to vent anger. Expressing anger in appropriate ways that don't alienate people is a healthy thing. But the act of venting, in and of itself, is overrated. A person with a chronic anger problem can vent all day and then get up the next morning and do it again. He has something going on inside that he needs to deal with, and it's going to require "more than counting to ten," as a colleague of mine, Kay Yerkovich, once said.

To look at how anger works, let's return to the example of Alan and his direct report. As it happened, Alan's anger was a normal reaction to an external situation. But it could have been different. Suppose, for example, the manager was working fine and wasn't causing any problems. But Alan was constantly finding himself annoyed when he talked to him. That might point to something inside Alan, an alert of a different nature. It might have been that the man had some trait or style that was a hot button for Alan. Say he was somewhat chatty, and Alan liked people to get to the point. There would be nothing wrong with the person, but Alan just didn't like that style. In that case, the action step would probably be a different one, something like understanding where that annoyance came from. Maybe Alan had a previous boss who never got down to brass tacks and Alan couldn't get clarity from him, and that experience stayed with him. Then, having understood the source, Alan could forgive that previous boss, let it go, and find more tolerance for his direct report.

It could also go the other way. Suppose the manager was a very direct and to-the-point person while Alan preferred a little conversation before getting to matters. The direct report would seem cold and abrupt to him. Then Alan would have to figure out why he reacted negatively to that style. The point here is simply that your anger may be about the situation, or it may be about you. As a leader, you need to be open to either option. Just remember the problem-solving nature of anger. Don't avoid it. Don't let it control you. Be sure to find its source, and take action.

Anger is a signal to take action, but it's important to acknowledge that there may be times when there is nothing we can do to fix the problem. Anger may have helped us to work hard to resolve things, but some matters, no matter how hard we try, don't always go how we want. We can't solve every problem and we can't win 100 percent of the time. I believe we can win a great deal of the time, but anyone who says we can bat a thousand doesn't live in the real world.

In these cases, your anger may have done its job and run its course. When you have done everything you know to do, been as creative as possible, received lots of sound advice, gone the third mile, persisted, and prayed, then it may be time to move past anger and problem-solving. Otherwise, the anger only serves to keep you frustrated and beating your head against the wall.

This is the situation of the leader who continues being annoyed about something he needs to let go of. He brings up an unchangeable problem over and over again. It takes over his thoughts like an obsession, and his colleagues get tired of hearing about it. He is stuck in what psychologists call a *protest stance*. He is still arguing his side in his mind and unable to get past it. You will often hear this person say things such as, "It can't be; it shouldn't be; maybe if I try it this way," about a situation that won't change. He is protesting a situation he needs to let go of. His anger is driving him to continue fighting, but it is not a wise use of his anger. Instead, it may be time for him to change, adapt, and go in another direction. And that sort of protest anger has its final resolution in the next emotion I want to address, which is sadness. It is not the most popular emotion for leaders, but it is a vital one to experience and understand.

Sadness: I Need to Grieve a Loss So I Can Move On

Sadness is a feeling of grief and mourning. We feel despondent or regretful. We shed tears and sometimes isolate ourselves. Sadness has its own signal and message, which is that we are experiencing loss. Something or someone we value and care about has left us. It's all about the process of grieving.

There are many victories and many losses you will experience in life and in leadership. That's just the way life is, and it's normal. A deal you dreamed of doesn't come through, no matter how hard you tried to make it work. A person who is driving you crazy will not listen to reason and persists in disruptive behavior. Market forces turn everything upside down, and things beyond your control derail your work. A window of opportunity you didn't take advantage of is now forever closed to you. You made a judgment call, and it turned out to be the wrong one.

On a more personal level, there are also many losses leaders experience. A marriage ends. A loved one passes away. Your children go down the wrong path and cause you heartache. You make mistakes in how you treat people you love, and you alienate them. You encounter health problems. You develop a bad habit that you regret. You wonder where God is, in all of this, and if he cares.

As a leader, you may be tempted to skip over this section on sadness. Using sadness in leadership likely seems counterintuitive to the whole purpose of your leadership, which is to effectively move your people and your organization forward in some way. Leaders focus on adding value and achieving outcomes. What value and what outcomes can arise from being sad? Doesn't that lead to slowing down, stagnation, a pity party, blaming, and even depression? Isn't it better to keep moving, cut your losses, and keep positive?

In my work with leaders over time, I have come to understand this perspective. Leaders are under tremendous pressure to be an example, an inspiration, a positive force, and a source of energy to their organization. That is the reality, and it is the right thing. It is an essential of leadership.

At the same time, there is another essential, and that is to be able to handle losses, as well as the corresponding emotion of sadness, for they will happen. Loss is part of life, the way the world is.

Losses have three sources: you, others, and the world. Your own failures and lapses in judgment can cause a loss. Others in your life can be the source of a loss. And sometimes, the economy, the weather, or an illness that is no one's fault can cause a loss. More often than not, the losses you experience are some combination of the three. The point is this: as a leader, you *will* lose. It is a fact. How a leader deals with loss separates the winners from the losers. Ironically, those who can't deal with loss ultimately lose. And those who know how to deal with loss will win. Here is how that works.

Sadness is the emotional signal of the reality of loss. It says, *I lost. Maybe someone else won, maybe not, but I know I lost. And I lost something I wanted.* Whether you lost a position, a venture, a financial gain, or a relationship, sadness connects you with whatever you wanted. It is about desiring something, most likely something good. And desire—wanting something, feeling a longing for something—is the prerequisite for sadness and grief. If you don't desire or care about anything, you will never have to feel sadness. There is nothing to lose, so there is nothing to let go of.

People who are detached from their desires, their hearts, and their relationships are often spared of feeling sad. But that is not a good way to live. In fact, very detached people often suffer from relational problems, intimacy issues, and clinical depression. Not wanting or caring about something, for the purpose of avoiding sadness, is to miss the point of leadership in the first place. Leadership is about wanting to make a difference, having a vision, helping people you care about, changing lives, and meeting goals. Desire and care keep you moving forward on that path. You can't have one without the other. That means you must allow desire and sadness to coexist in your inner life.

So what good is sadness then? Here is its value: *Sadness tells you to let go and move on.* It points you to the reality that you can't have something you desire, at least today, and you need to go another route. Give up trying to put a square peg in a round hole. Stop trying to make the deal work that can't work. Realize that person is the wrong one for the job, though you desperately need someone in that position. If you have a guy in your small group who wants to leave, and you've had several conversations to try to work it out, let him leave and wish him well. Set a goal this next year that is more realistic than the one last year that was impossible.

There is tremendous value in paying attention to your sad feelings. It keeps you from becoming stuck like the leader I mentioned before, who was lost in an endless cycle of "It can't be; it shouldn't be; maybe if I try it this way . . ." That begins to sound like a love-smitten guy who, when rejected, starts stalking his ex. You don't want that kind of existence. It isn't the path to success.

Perhaps the main reason leaders have a particularly tough time with this emotion is that *sadness means you are helpless to change some reality.* That doesn't mean you are completely and totally helpless. Certainly you have options and choices, but there are times you must accept that you are helpless to change someone or something. For example, you might be helpless in

- changing someone's negative opinion of you.
- resurrecting a deal that has gone away.
- convincing someone to stay who wants to leave.
- keeping a position that has been eliminated.
- undoing or diminishing the consequences of an unfortunate choice.

Leaders resist helpless situations; it's not what they signed up for in leadership. That is understandable. Leaders are workers and doers. But as I said, acknowledging sadness isn't equivalent to complete and total helplessness. It has limits and parameters. You can always go another way to achieve what you want to achieve. In fact, sadness is a reminder of an important truth: *You are not God.* That's a good reality to become accustomed to! You do not have the power to make everything go your way all of the time. Your sadness points you to a consigned and limited helplessness that will help you face your loss, let it go, and move on to those matters in which you can be helpful and effective.

During the past several years, Dr. Henry Cloud and I have conducted a weeklong training experience for leaders called the Ultimate Leadership Workshop.[1] In these workshops, Henry and I teach the attendees principles on leadership, values, the internal world, and achieving outcomes. One component of the week is that the leaders participate in small groups, which provide a safe place to process what they're learning, unpack themselves, and get real. It's where the information they are learning makes that eighteen-inch journey from their heads to their hearts.

One of the biggest takeaways attendees tell us about in their feedback is that they gain a new respect for the value of sadness. Now, these are highly motivated, competent, values-driven, and accomplished people.

But they, inevitably, did not have the skills to handle loss. No one had ever helped them with that aspect of life, work, and leadership. They say things like:

- "I've been holding on to a demand to be perfect in all things. I'm learning to let that image go, as it will never happen. I'm learning that excellence doesn't demand perfection, and I have a new perspective."
- "I thought I could keep everyone in my company happy if I tried hard enough. I've let it go, and I'm becoming free of that trap."
- "I've had some business failures that I could not stop beating myself up about. I've allowed myself to feel the sadness, and now I can see them instead as learning experiences for my future."
- "I miss my team in my previous job, and I'm letting the sadness happen so that I can move on. Now I have more energy and encouragement to continue with the new group."
- "I've had some relational losses, and I never let myself say good-bye emotionally. I never got over that person, and it affected my work. I've now gone through the grief, and I'm back to my old self."

Sadness can help you move on to new opportunities and new challenges. Though it is a negative emotion, it has positive benefits. I talked to an executive who had transitioned from one company to another. When I asked him how it was going, he said, "I like the company I'm with, but I haven't really been excited about it or engaged there."

"Any idea why?" I asked.

"I realized that I transitioned very quickly," he said. "I was with my former company for a long time, and I had a lot of relationships and experiences there. I don't think I ever gave myself time to let it go and grieve it."

From a time and resource perspective, sadness has a good return on investment. It is a temporary process. It finishes and resolves. It allows you to free up energy and motivation in your mind to lead the way you want to. And it helps you learn invaluable lessons from the past.

Sometimes I will talk to leaders who have no value for sadness. "Just get over it," they say. I can understand that in some cases. For example, if someone is complaining endlessly about a situation that is long past and is yesterday's news, they do need to get over it. Or, if their sadness concerns a problem that isn't a big issue, they need to get over it. That is true about matters that don't really matter to you. You change an office in the same building. You train for a new specialty. These are changes that simply require adaptation and flexibility. They don't tend to generate a lot of sadness because there's not a significant loss involved. Or if some failure you experience isn't a big deal, you just dust yourself off and get back on the horse.

However, sometimes "just getting over it" will make things worse for you over time. If you have lost something or someone truly important to you, you will most likely have sadness about the loss. It's best to honor it by allowing some time to be sad. It will do you good, and enable you to move on from there without carrying unnecessary baggage.

Stay up-to-date on your grief and losses. Don't let them go unattended for a long time. The sooner you grieve a loss, the less time it will take to let it go. It may be a couple of minutes, say if you're disappointed because someone you had a dinner appointment with, whom you were looking forward to being with, had to cancel. If it's a significant loss, it will be much longer. But the longer you avoid the grief, the longer it will take to finally finish it and move on. Jump into the grief process, and you will jump back into normal life that much sooner.

Productive Grief: How to Let Go and Move On

Here is a practical guide to give you the basic steps of handling grief intentionally.

- *Identify the loss.* Grief points to a loss in your past or present, and can be about a lost opportunity, relationship, or a failure.
- *Assess the impact.* The greater the impact, the greater the need to grieve. Missing an exit on the highway is a low-impact loss, but losing an important relationship is a high-impact loss.
- *Create a receptive environment.* It's hard to feel your sadness in

the middle of a team meeting or while making a sales pitch. Set aside a few minutes to be alone or perhaps talk with a safe person who is warm and accepting.

- *Allow sad feelings and tears.* These should simply emerge, as they are just the emotional reflection of the impact the loss had on you.
- *Learn the lesson.* Reflect on what you may have learned from the loss and move on. It might be about how to make a decision or how to handle a relational conflict the next time.

Guilt and Shame: I Need to Accept Myself—Not Condemn Myself—for My Mistakes

Leaders screw up—that is simply a reality. The best leaders not only learn from their screw-ups, they don't allow guilt and shame to disrupt their effectiveness. If you don't take time to understand and deal with them, the emotions of guilt and shame will sap your energy, tank your motivation, and gut your creativity. Though guilt and shame are different in a technical sense, they are best described broadly as *an attack on yourself, by yourself.* You condemn or judge yourself harshly for violating a standard, for failing, for letting someone down, for not being sufficient, or for hurting someone, to name a few infractions. Further, this attack on yourself can be about something that is either true or simply perceived. You can beat yourself up, for example, and condemn yourself as a loser for hitting a triple instead of a homer.

Guilt and shame are often expressions of self-judgment. Here are a few examples that leaders experience:

I don't know what I'm doing in this job. I'm a loser.
If people knew how incompetent I really am, I'd be gone.
My last mistake really hurt a lot of people.
I'm always disappointing people and letting them down.
I give up too easily.
I never learn anything from what people are trying to tell me.
The organization's struggles are all my fault.

It doesn't take a lot of these self-attacking statements to cause great discouragement and even paralysis in a leader. But it is a common struggle that many leaders experience. So as we're dealing with our emotions, instead of trying to ignore or get rid of guilt and shame feelings, we need to understand their signal function so we can chart the way to resolving them.

There is nothing wrong with feeling bad when you fail. It means that you live in reality. When you succeed, you should celebrate. When you err, having negative feelings like disappointment, remorse, and concern for others shows you care about people, your responsibilities, and your leadership. Have you ever talked to someone who made huge mistakes that cost the organization a lot of money, and the person shrugged it off with, "Oh, well, it will be better next time"? I have, and I don't trust these people with my time or my money. They aren't people who consider their accountability to others to be a grave matter. They are problem people. They are not examples of healthy, guilt-free living.

Guilt and shame are much worse than being disappointed or remorseful. They keep you in a vicious cycle of reliving the past, self-recriminations, and leadership paralysis. When you experience these feelings, you need to look at what is going on. Most of the time, these emotions are signaling one of several issues, each of which has a corresponding action step. For example:

- Your standards are unrealistic and need to be modified and adapted to what is realistically achievable.
- You are overidentifying with your error and think that it defines who you are as a person, rather than being simply a mistake that you, a normally competent person, have made.
- You have a deficit of accepting, safe, loving relationships with people who can help you feel loved and okay about yourself, and you need a few of these around you.
- You create parent figures out of the people around you and imagine that they are more disappointed in you than they actually are. You need to talk to them about how they really see you.
- You take too much responsibility for the job, the results, and

everything in between so that when there is a failure, it's all your fault. You need to bear your own burden of leadership and be responsible for yourself while at the same time allowing others to take responsibility for themselves.

As you can see, these issues can slow down your progress and growth as a leader. But these action steps can take you a long way toward ending self-attacks and replacing them with loving self-correction that we can all use and benefit from.

As we've dealt with anxiety, anger, sadness, and guilt and shame, it's important to know that I am describing *normal* experiences of these emotions, along with *normal* action steps that resolve them. Sometimes, however, these emotions can become very intense and painful, and sometimes they do not resolve over time. If you are following these recommendations and find that the feelings are still disrupting your life with no relief over time, it may be that the issue they are signaling is deeper or more serious than you thought. That means you may have a clinical problem, in which there is an injury or emotional deficit that needs professional help and healing with a good psychologist. I know many leaders from all over the world who have received great personal benefit from psychotherapy and have found that their work and results improve as well.

Positive Emotions

Now I want to explore three of the primary positive emotions that leaders experience. Again, just as all emotions do, positive feelings function as a signal to you; they aren't ends in themselves. So it is just as important with positive emotions as it is with the negative ones to understand what they mean for you and your leadership.

Warmth: I Am Drawn to Be with This Person

Warmth is a feeling that draws you to move toward people you care about and engage with them. Warmth can exist in any sort of relationship:

romantic, friendship, or family. It simply is an emotion that makes you want to be close to or in the presence of another person. It can lead you to a satisfying conversation with your spouse, a great time playing with your kids, a stimulating night with your date, or a jog with a friend. Warmth reconnects you to people.

As a leader, you may be tempted to think, *If it's not broke, don't fix it. Why analyze warmth? Just enjoy it.* It is certainly an emotion to be appreciated and experienced, no doubt about it. But there is also value in understanding what warmth is telling you. Basically, warm feelings signal that this person is bringing you good. That is, he or she is providing some things for you that you need, some part of the relational fuel that you will need in some form for the rest of your life. The warmth helps you pay attention to that fuel so that you don't neglect it.

Think about the last good meal you ate in a restaurant. Most likely, that thought motivates you to make plans to return. The meal brought good fuel to you. Warm feelings remind you to get back to the connections you have.

As you most likely know, leaders are somewhat vulnerable to being workaholics or too task-oriented. Business demands and schedules can take up huge amounts of time. It is easy to run on fumes and become detached from the people you need and who also need you. Warm feelings remind you of the importance of relationships. They make you want to connect, to talk, to be intimate, and to care for someone who, in turn, cares for you. In my own work, when I am flying to speak at a conference, I often find myself thinking of the people I'll be speaking to, and how I hope they will benefit from the content I'll be delivering. Feeling an alliance with the audience helps me to get my focus off myself and onto how to help their lives and careers. That's an example of warmth in action on a personal level.

In terms of organizational work, I have repeatedly witnessed how the absence or presence of warmth affects a team's functioning or the entire culture of an organization. A client of mine who ran a large firm was a very nice guy, with high integrity and care for his people, but didn't have what you might call a great bedside manner. I don't mean that he should have spent hours being *Kumbaya* with his people, but he needed to soften his highly-task-based relational style. Too often, when he talked to anyone on his team, he went directly into task mode: "Did you finish the Smith analysis?" No greeting, no preamble, no interest in the other person. While his people respected his integrity and values, they were always a bit anxious when he showed up at their office. My client was surprised and distressed when I gave him this feedback. He did two things to fix this: (1) He started taking just a minute or two to chat for a bit by asking his team members about how their day was going or what their kids were up to; (2) He periodically asked people to coffee or lunch with no work agenda. Even without him expressing warmth, the company was already successful, but when he made these changes, performance and teamwork increased even more. His team felt like they had a "new boss."

If warm feelings aren't something you experience on some sort of regular basis, consider that a problem. We certainly have to work, focus, concentrate, strategize, problem-solve, motivate, and inspire. These are the task-based parts of leadership. But if there aren't also some moments during the day when you have warm feelings, you need to consider a few possibilities. One is that you don't have enough of a support system in your life (we will deal with this in more depth in part 4), so you are somewhat detached and disconnected. Another is that you have difficulty letting people in or trusting them emotionally, so you cut off the warm feelings in order to stay safe from hurt. This may indicate a need for professional counseling, to help you learn to open up safely. Another possibility is that you place a high value on task completion and a low value on relationships; you are more comfortable doing than relating. If this is the case, you may need to reorient your values so that, while performance must always be the key, relationship is a close and necessary second.

Satisfaction: I Feel That This Was Very Much Worth the Effort

Satisfaction is an emotion that relates to work, accomplishment, and performance. It is a feeling of contentment that we have completed a task we are proud of. We can look back at the achievement and say to ourselves, *This was very much worth the effort.*

Leaders enjoy and relish those moments. They are a quiet celebration and reflection on the effort it took and the results that were produced. You may feel satisfied with a positive quarterly earnings statement, a building project that is now complete, a project your team did well, or a tough problem in your small group that you helped someone come through and have a better life.

What does satisfaction signal? I believe this emotion points out two things for you. The first is that you can stop now! Work and leadership need closure. There should be some points at which you know that a task is done, whether it took five minutes or five years. You can't keep up the pace, nonstop, without satisfaction telling you that you can rest and turn the page. When leaders don't experience satisfaction, they often become driven and frenetic. They are productive, to some extent, but it's ultimately a recipe for exhaustion and misery.

The other direction that satisfaction points us to is that work and leadership should bring a measure of fulfillment and joy. Your success should be a cause for satisfaction. The emotion then serves as a sign that life can be good and also that you can continue down the track to the next challenge. Without that emotion, work could become drudgery. Satisfaction is a signal that you are producing something worthwhile and will continue to do so.

A company I worked with had a big payday after a few years of strategic work. The CEO was committed to sharing her satisfaction with her team. She celebrated the achievement by giving out a substantial bonus and a trip to a resort area. Her team is one of the most loyal I've ever seen.

Happiness: I Have a Sense of Well-Being and Contentment
While satisfaction is the feeling associated with results and accomplishment, happiness is the emotion that is concerned with anything good that happens to you. It has nothing to do with whether or not you accomplished anything. That is, happiness is a sense of well-being and contentment in general.

Of all the emotions you have, happiness is the one that is most dependent on your circumstances and least dependent on you as a person. It is basically a response to positive things happening: a job you enjoy, a marriage that is fulfilling, a child who is doing well, a charity you are involved with, a hobby that is fun, good weather, a good meal, a funny movie. Happy feelings simply go with happy events. It doesn't take a lot of character or maturity to feel happy when happy things happen.

There are some dispositionally happy people. They simply have a positive emotional outlook. They are not bothered by things that bother other people. It's not that they are in denial or are pretending inside; they really feel that way. Most of the time, it is because they have experienced a long pattern of significant loving and secure relationships. Those experiences tend to provide a happier viewpoint. But that is not our focus here, as we are dealing more with the pure feeling of happiness itself.

How does understanding happiness apply to your life as a leader? What is your takeaway? The first is to look at what made you happy for those few minutes and *be grateful for that event*. Gratitude means that you appreciate what just happened to you. You don't dismiss it, ignore it, or take it for granted. You don't say, "Well, what's next?" and move on. You experience thankfulness for it. You tell people who were involved in the event how much you appreciate them. There really is something to the "stop and smell the roses" thinking. People who don't take time to feel happy about blessings in their lives are headed for regrets and even isolation from others.

The second takeaway is that happiness serves as a reinforcement to continue whatever we are doing. If being around supportive and interesting people makes you happy, you will probably find them again. If researching a marketing concept is enjoyable, you will probably continue in that track. Happiness reinforces whatever caused it in the first place. Hopefully, what brought you happy feelings is also something healthy, valuable, and good for you as well.

The third takeaway is that people will follow happiness in you as their leader more than they will follow your unhappiness. If you are aware of and appreciative of the good going around, happiness will be contagious to those who follow you. They can always go somewhere else to work or help out, but people naturally gravitate toward the positive. Again, I'm not talking about putting on some idealistic pretense of happiness. Happy leaders are also honest, authentic, direct, and realistic.

These traits all go together without conflict. In fact, happy individuals tend not to be aware that they are happy. They just are. If someone asks them, "Are you happy in what you are doing?" they may have to think about it, and then say, "I guess I am!"

I have a friend who worked for many years in a high-level corporate position. She was happy there and was very successful. She left for a while to do some other activities. However, when she got an offer to jump back in at a CEO level with a new venture, she took it. We were talking about her decision, and she said, "Once I decided to go, I called several people who had been on the old team with me, to recruit them. When I told them about the new company, they were ready to go. The old company had been such a great experience for all of us."

I was reminded of the movie *Ocean's Eleven*. Danny Ocean recruits his old friends to plan a major crime, and the team comes together to execute it. Like Danny, my friend had no trouble bringing her old group back together. They had caught the *happiness bug* from her and knew that her happiness would become their happiness as well.

The fourth takeaway is that a lack of happiness can be a signal that you need to make changes. If you are miserable in your job, make whatever changes you can make to improve things. If you aren't happy as a leader, find out if there is some skill or competency or coaching that would help. This doesn't mean we are to interpret every negative feeling as a sign that something is going wrong. A tough and direct conversation between two people in a company can be very uncomfortable and not particularly happy, but it can bring great good. The point is, pay attention to unhappiness and trace it to its origin, just as you are to do with every emotion.

Having said all this, I must now warn you: *Happiness is a valuable experience, but it is a miserable goal.* Take it off your goal list and replace it with something else. In its proper place, as a celebration of gratitude and an appreciation of the good, the emotion of happiness has real benefit. It is a fruit, a result of the good. But it never works out when we focus on happiness as something to accomplish. I hear this a lot from leaders: "I just want to be happy in my life." I certainly understand the desire, but happiness as your ultimate goal will lead nowhere, and even to worse than nowhere. It can lead to problems in life and leadership.

To reach your most important goals in life, you will have to experience unhappiness. What is really important in life—and in your intuitive leadership—has to do with the values we explored in part 1. These values bring meaning and purpose to life. They are larger than you, they existed before you did, and they will continue long after you are gone. They make life make sense to you. And they will require diligence, conflict, heated debate, confrontation, delaying gratification, patience, failure, perseverance, and labor. No one who builds a great organization, leads people to a worthy goal, crafts a successful marriage, or launches competent kids does so without some significant measure of unhappiness along the way. But for people who undertake a life of meaning and purpose, losing some happiness along the way is a small price to pay. The eventual achievement and results bring all the happiness they need in the end.

Here is another way to think about it. There are two major demographics of people who are focused on happiness as their goal—children and addicts. Both live for the pleasure of the moment. They want to feel good. They want positive things to happen to them. They avoid negatives and unhappiness. And they are unable to say no to their desires. For them, the only time period is the now. Their goal in life is to be happy.

Children need parents who teach them that the best way to live is to learn to love and to take responsibility for their lives. Gradually, they extend their demand for pleasure and instant happiness into meaningful goals and habits. Addicts need professionals who will support them in their struggle, help them find insight and healing, and teach them that developing self-control and delaying gratification will help restore the lives they lost.

Certainly, as a leader, you should appreciate happiness when it comes and model happiness for your people. But also look for the greater themes—the things that make life matter to all humans—such as healthy relationships, purpose, and meaning, rather than mere happiness.

There is something interesting about happiness that I have noticed: *When you stop trying to find happiness, it will find you.* I don't mean this in some mysterious way. There is reality to this idea. When you focus on what is really important, and live and lead in ways that are congruent with your values, you will experience the side benefit of happiness. It will find you in those moments of enjoyment along the way. And it will also find you when you see that a life well lived is a good life indeed.

Focus and Act

If you want to be an effective leader, you need to elevate your emotional world to the same status as your thinking world. Feelings aren't for kids and weak moments. They are powerful instruments to help you navigate your challenges and the path of your team, group, or organization. So use the information and skills in this chapter to be intentional, that is, to focus on your emotions and act on the data they provide. That is how you will experience the highest level of benefit.

Not long ago, I was talking to a student in the program I lead at the Townsend Institute for Leadership and Counseling, who told me this story: "I've been using what you've taught about emotions in the workplace in the HR department I lead. My boss started to notice that I've been able to solve several complicated conflicts between employees, all of which involved paying attention to emotions. When I told my boss that I learned these skills at the Institute, he said, 'I'm paying for the rest of your tuition.'" It was another great example of how the feeling world is critical to the workplace.

It's also important to remember that being tuned in to the emotional world is part of the big picture of being intuitive and leading from your gut. You need to listen and pay attention to your internal world, as well as the metrics that come your way, to be an effective leader.

Next, we'll focus on understanding and harnessing an emotion that is so significant to your leadership it deserves its own chapter: passion. Leading with passion will change everything for you.

Chapter 7

THE PURSUIT OF PASSION

I was flying to a speaking engagement one day and engaged in conversation with the man sitting next to me. When I asked him what he did for a living, he said, "I'm a commercial pilot."

"I understand that takes quite a bit of training," I said.

"It does require a lot of training," he replied, "school, military service, noncommercial planes, the whole nine yards. But it's been worth it. I like my career."

Curious, I asked, "So how did you decide on flying as your career? Did you go through some sort of focusing, search, or process of elimination from other areas?"

"No," he said. "It wasn't like that at all. I just had a passion for flying. Since I was a young kid, flying is all I've wanted to do. There was no need to eliminate anything because there was nothing else I even considered."

I was struck by his statement and thought about it for a long time. Here was a man who, for whatever reason, had a passion inside him that hadn't wavered for decades. A passion that motivated him to accomplish years of rigorous training toward his career goal.

Since it took me a long time, with different redirections, to finally find my own passion and career, I felt a twinge of envy for his clear and early focus. Some people find their passion earlier in life; others take more time. But the point is that you, as a leader, must experience some sort of a passion for your work. It will make all the difference between creating an "okay" organization and an exciting one.

Imagine asking a couple friends what they thought of a movie they just saw. If your friends say, "It was okay," it's pretty much guaranteed you're not going to rush to the movie theater and buy a ticket. But if your friends say, "Wow! It was incredible," you're much more likely to make it part of your Friday night plans. The first response is sometimes referred to as "damning with faint praise," and it is a serious buzzkill.

I have worked with CEOs who unwittingly damned their new initiatives with faint praise. They had no passion, and everyone could see they were not emotionally engaged. When we worked together on accessing their own internal passion, the team and the culture improved.

Three Things You Need to Know about Passion

The clearest way to understand the role of passion for your leadership is to explore three things: *what passion is,* so you can identify it in yourself and others; *where passion comes from,* so you can understand its nature and what makes it work; and *how to get it* (or get more of it), so you have action steps to develop passion.

What Is Passion?

I define *passion* simply as "focused desire," or "desire with direction." Passion is an emotion of great clarity. It is something you feel. You can talk about passion, and you can think about passion, but deep down, you feel it. It harnesses your interest and desire for something and points them in a specific direction.

There are countless passions leaders may have, as many as there are leadership interests. Some have a passionate drive for a web-based company. For some, it's retail. For others, it may be a communications venture, or health care. Some want a growing church. Others want to lead a happy family or a meaningful small group.[1]

As with any emotion, passion also has a purpose and a role. Passion drives you in a specific direction so you will be unwavering and clear. It moves you to keep going, to make the sacrifices necessary, to continue on the path because you are in the right place at the right time. Like happiness, passion is a positive and pleasurable emotion. However, it is much more focused and specific than happiness. You might say you are happy leading the IT department of your company. That may be a very good thing, but it may also mean that you can easily find happiness doing something else. But if you say you have a passion for leading the IT department, it means it's about your mission, something about which you could say, *This is part of who I am.* That means it would be much more difficult for you to find that passion elsewhere.

Imagine if someone were to say to you, "Three years ago, I had a passion for marketing. Two years ago, I fell in love with administration. Last year, I was all about accounting. And this year, I am passionate about sales." You would think that that person was either unbalanced or disingenuous, and you would probably be right. Who would want to be led by that person? Leaders with passion not only create interest, but they create security because their passion is real, dependable, and reliable. It's not a flavor-of-the-month emotion. Passion stays focused like a laser beam; it keeps you on target and tends to last for a long time in your life if it is the real thing.

That doesn't mean that passion *never* changes. People's passions can change as their life seasons move on, and that is simply because the individuals themselves are changing. A client of mine who was extremely successful in his business for twenty years found himself increasingly attracted to doing business in the music world. He stayed connected on a board level to his company, but began to make relationships in a totally different industry.

This developmental view of passion is very different from the "different passion per year" problem I described above. My client played out his first passion and did very well. So many "flavor of the year" passion people are actually individuals who are simply struggling to stick with something long enough to become successful.

So what does passion do for you as a leader? It makes the long-haul work of leadership engaging and enjoyable. When I was in high school, I was a distance runner. I wasn't very good, but I enjoyed it enough that I could say it was a passion. When I went for a practice run alone and got tired, I found there were four things I could do to keep myself from getting bored or going crazy. First, I would look into the distance, down the road, to see where I would end up. But that could be discouraging because the horizon took so long to change, and I couldn't see progress fast enough. Second, I would look at the road in front of me where my feet were going. That was okay for a while because I could tell I was getting somewhere. But that, too, would get tiresome as I saw just thousands of steps—left, right, left, right—and it reduced me to counting them in some obsessive way, which was no fun. The third choice was that I would think about something else in my life: my buddies, my girlfriend, my family, sports, music. But sooner or later, the physical pain of running would get in the way. The fourth option turned out to be the best for me: I noticed what was going on around me. I looked at the scenery, the road, and the houses. And I noticed my breathing, muscle movements, and the feel of the sun on my skin. When I anchored myself to the present, time passed faster for me, and I actually enjoyed myself.

That is what passion does for you. In your lifetime, you will spend a lot of time working with people you are leading. You may spend the time thinking only about the goal and miss the moment. You may check the hours off on a spreadsheet, and be reduced to counting steps. You may zone out and think about things you enjoy, that you would rather be doing right now, and not be present. Or passion can keep you engaged, right now, in doing something that requires hard work, but at the same time is rewarding *and provides a worthwhile outcome in the future.* With passion, you gain both a present and a future benefit. It is the best way to go.

To clarify, there are certainly people who are what you might call *passionate people.* Whatever they are into, they are into it 110 percent. I would describe these people as enthusiastic or intense, and that can be a very good thing. But that is not what I am describing here. Our view of passion for the purposes of this book is related to what you do, particularly as it relates to your leadership. It is a focused desire to do what you are doing as a leader.

Where Does Passion Come From?

Passion develops when you are doing what you are designed to do. In other words, there is an intersection between who you really are and what you are involved in. There are two elements here, the external and the internal. The external activity may be a job, a project, a position, a career. But that activity is a trigger that reaches deep inside, and who you really are, your real self, responds to that. You may have thoughts about it, such as, *This intrigues me,* or *I want to try that some more,* or *I could be pretty good at that.* But the emotion that corresponds to those thoughts is passion. And when you feel passion, you will most likely find ways to get more deeply involved in that activity.

In reality, then, you can't be passionate about every work or leadership context. Human beings are not designed to be able to do everything. That's not how life works. You have certain abilities, traits, styles, and gifts. They form some niche that makes you the best fit for that area. Your task is to find that niche and fit it to the activity.

Once passion exists, most people know it. It's a little like falling in love, which makes sense because there is passion in that arena as well. You don't have to make yourself get involved in the work. You find yourself thinking about it, being curious about it, bringing it up in your conversations. Discipline helps passion, but discipline is not a substitute for passion.

For example, I have a friend who is highly placed in the real estate industry. When the real estate market was going through difficult times a few years ago, my friend was in a position that required leading, training, and motivating a lot of people. When I asked him how it was going for him during that season, he said, "These are tough times. I have to make a lot of hard decisions every day. But I still wake up in the morning thinking about new ways to keep us moving and to keep my people productive. I love being in real estate, and I love working with my team. That is what makes me tick." That's a great example of true passion—it comes from deep inside a person and isn't derailed by difficult circumstances. In fact, as great leaders know, difficult circumstances can actually trigger your passion, remind you of who you are and what you're about, and help you persevere. Passion is the "go to" place when you are in times of challenge.

How Do We Get Passion?

Perhaps you can identify with my friend in the real estate business. You love what you do and even when you're not doing it, you're daydreaming about it, whether it's running your department, team, company, church, or small group. You don't have to write on your daily to-do list, "Think about how to keep my people motivated." It's there, in your inner world. If this is you, and if your passion is the right fit—meaning you have the abilities and strengths—you are fortunate. Keep on track.

However, if you feel like you haven't yet found your passion, or that perhaps it's time for a new one, there are some things you can do to move toward it. If you lead, you actually need two passions: *a passion for something you do well and are competent in,* and *a passion to lead others in that arena.* There is an order to this: your own passion first, your leadership passion second. You have to begin with yourself because if you don't love something, there is no way, over time, you will be able to lead others in it. You may be able to manage, guide, and assist them. But you cannot help your people to be inspired, excited, and productive when you don't have the juice yourself.

Imagine that someone came to you and said, "I'd like to be a leader." One of the questions you would probably ask would be, "So what do you do?" If the person's answer was, "Nothing in particular. I just want to lead people," you would likely not be considering how to find a place for that person on your team. Instead, you would probably say something like this: "Learn to be really good at something, and then come back, and let's talk." Who wants to be led by someone whose only passion is leading others . . . in what?

One exception to this might be corporate executives who have formal training and experience in leading a company. They have the capacity, from years of work, to go from leading a company in one industry to leading one in a completely different area. Their passion for doing something well may be the same as their passion for leading others, which is what corporate executives do. But most corporate executives are highly multi-competent people. They have a deep understanding of finances, marketing, accounting, strategies, human resources, and the like. So even they must start with themselves and then move to leadership.

Remember the pilot I talked to who was so passionate about his work? Follow his lead by first considering what you love, what you enjoy doing, and what you like because of the nature of the thing itself. This is the internal part. It may be teaching, administration, building, computers, selling, art, music, or theology. Look not only to today but also to the past and your patterns. What, in your life history, has been a focused desire? This is not a time to think of practicalities, such as *I can't quit my day job for this* or *I'm not talented in this*. These may be important considerations, but you can't put them first—it's the wrong sequence. Finding what you love to do, in your heart, must come first. Practical realities must come second.

Second, get experience. This is the external part. Talk to people, try things out, explore opportunities—however you do it, get experience in the area of your passion. The more active, frequent, and varied the experience, the more you will be able to attach to something that makes sense. The real you is waiting to be discovered, and your task is to find lots of different experiences that the real you will connect with and then trigger the passion. That is the basic formula to discovering and harnessing your passion: *look inside, and then go out and try things.*

Then do the same with leadership. Find out what you love about leadership and get the experience. People with a passion for leadership understand what drives them: seeing lives change, seeing the effects of teamwork on a project, helping people achieve what they normally couldn't, casting vision, solving problems. And they look for contexts to operate in: corporate, charity, family, personal growth, church. That part is simply a numbers game, one of gaining valuable experiences.

Obstacles to Identifying and Sustaining Passion

If you've identified what you love and worked to get the experience you need but still find it difficult to identify or sustain a laser-like experience of passion, it may be that you've got an obstacle to overcome. Here are some of the ones I've seen many leaders encounter, as well as some steps to help you resolve them.

A Dependency on Willpower

Since leaders are often highly disciplined and structured, they sometimes try to *will* their passion. That is, they work very hard at something they think they *should* have passion about. They diligently study it, go to trainings, get mentors, get themselves psyched up, and sincerely try to create a passion. And that is the problem. You can't create passion you don't have or force yourself to feel it. You simply must find it. It's just the way we are made as humans.

I have a friend who was at the top of his game in the insurance industry. He owned a small company and was highly successful. By all accounts, you would have thought he had a passion for what he was doing. He did, for the insurance business in general. But he didn't have a passion for the role he was in. He worked for many years as the owner, but he didn't enjoy the burdens owners have. Finally, and against conventional wisdom, he sold the business and went to work for a large insurance firm. He is at the top of his game there also, as their number one sales producer. He loves meeting people and he loves structuring solutions to complicated problems that help everyone involved. His competency levels haven't changed, but he now has a passion for his work. Why? Because he has a great support infrastructure and good resourcing that frees him up to focus on what he's best at, which is sales. He decided not to continue beating his head against the reality that he had no passion for owning the business. He listened to himself, to his experience, and to reality, and made the right move for himself.

I mention him because usually the story of passion tends to go in the other direction: the corporate person becomes a small business owner, an artist, a musician, or a minister. But my friend's example shows that you can't pick your passion. You can only find it. So don't try to "make yourself" have passion. Look for it. Use your willpower and discipline to keep you structured in the process of discovery.

An Idealized View of Passion

There are times when a person simply doesn't have the opportunity or options to live out her passion in her career. Sometimes there are other realities that prevent one's passion from being lived out, such as a medical condition that forces a job change, a passion that can't pay the bills as well as a current job, or an economy that necessitates taking a job that's not the best fit, for a period of time.

Certainly you need to pay attention to these realities. If you've tried your best, for a long time, and have searched diligently for a job in your area of passion, and if for some legitimate reason you can't experience passion in your current tasks, you may have to adapt and change. It's neither loving nor responsible to cause your family to struggle indefinitely while you go for your dream. If your dream has a fixed and short-term goal, like medical school or an MBA, that is different. Otherwise, your family should come first and be provided for.

This scenario often involves a limited view of passion that is highly idealistic. You believe that your job must ignite your passion. It is true that *something* should ignite your passions, but there are times when the job doesn't. So you look to other venues for that: working with kids, soup kitchens, hobbies, art, mentoring others, sports, and the like. People do that all the time, and many become accomplished leaders in their avocations because that is the context in which they can best live out their passion and help people.

Problems in Leaving Home Emotionally

Many leaders aren't able to access their passion because they have never finished the task of leaving home emotionally. They can't access their true self, who they really are, because that person isn't accessible yet. This is one of the core issues of leadership from the inner reality. You must lead from your reality and no one else's. That journey is yours alone.

As children, we were designed to receive compassion, safety, structure, and wisdom from loving parents. During that process, we identify with them and their passions. A little girl goes to work at Mom's office and plays with the computer, pretending to be her. A boy goes to the construction site where Dad works and uses a plastic hammer on the beams. This identification helps children to develop the skills and abilities to handle adult life. They see that work is a large part of life, that it is normal and enjoyable, meaningful and required. It's what people do.

Ultimately, children begin to be secure enough to develop their own passions, separate from that of their parents' passions. They are occupied by an interest or hobby that their parents may not have. Their parents encourage this interest, support it, and find ways to help their children grow in that passion. Then, when the children finally leave home, they are equipped to discover activities that will trigger their ultimate passion of task and career.

I will always be thankful to my parents, to whom this book is dedicated, for seeing their job as equipping their four kids, rather than telling them what to do. They encouraged us to try different things, from business to health care to artistic endeavors. They had no master plan for us. In fact, as adults, my three siblings and I have all lived in different states and pursued diverse careers and life paths. We care about one another and stay in touch, but we have each found our own places and passions. My mother once told me that her friends sometimes said to her, "Isn't it sad that your kids moved so far away?" Then she said, "My friends are sorry for me, but they don't understand. I do miss not seeing you all as much as I'd like, but I am so happy that you have found what you want in life."

That is how leaving home is supposed to happen. But sometimes, unknowingly, parents discourage their children from having ideas, feelings, and passions that are separate from their own. They think the child should follow in their footsteps. Or they may think the child should follow in some other path that they aren't on—*but it is still the parents' passion for the child, not the child's own passion.* And that is the problem. Your passion can come only from you. It can't be inherited.

The laborer will tell his child, "You should be a doctor; don't get your hands dirty like I had to." The corporate executive will say, "Start your own business; I never had enough independence." The business owner will say, "You love people so much; be a teacher." These approaches don't open doors to passion. They close them.

It gets especially troublesome if the parents resist the child being a separate person in other ways. For example, they may only be loving, caring, and supportive if the child is responsive, compliant, and positive with them. They treat the child's attempts to think differently, disagree, and have different interests as a lack of love and loyalty to them, and they may criticize, withdraw affection, manipulate, or become silent. The message gets through: *You are a Smith, and your passion is the Smiths' passion for you.*

Ultimately, young adults who emerge from such a family do not have a fully developed and authentic self, nor do they have access to a real passion. Instead, they follow the work and life path they think is best for them because that was what their parents encouraged. But over time, even though they may be very good at whatever it is they do, they can't own their career at the deepest level because their inner life has not yet left home. Emotionally, they are still fused with their parents.

I have worked with many leaders who have struggled with this issue. They came to me for guidance, thinking they had the wrong job. Then they found out that this was a premature diagnosis. They weren't yet equipped inside to know what the "right job" is. Their passion wasn't yet accessible. So they learn the process of growing up and becoming their own person. They learn to be more honest about what they think and feel, even if it isn't the family party line. They learn to honor their parents without obeying their parents. They learn to take risks and chances. And most of them, in time, finish the process, leave home successfully (again, this is internal though there are a few instances of them having to literally move out of the house!), and find both their own emotional life and their passion.

Having said this, there are also many examples of someone who follows the footsteps of a successful parent and does well with that. But usually at some point, there was a time in which that individual thought through and wrestled with the question, *Is this really me?*

You cannot overestimate how important leaving home emotionally and becoming your own person is to experiencing your passion. Then, and only then, can you find yourself and be the right person in the right place at the right time for your leadership.

An Inability to Tolerate Loss of Options

Sometimes people can't access their passion, even after trying lots of jobs and experiences. This is very discouraging to them. And time is not kind to these individuals. As they get older, they wonder if they will ever land on what they love, or if they are destined to keep going from one beginning point to another, over and over again. These people genuinely struggle, and it is hard for them to stay motivated and encouraged.

Often, they are highly competent and, more importantly, *multital-ented* people. The multitalented part is important here. They are good with people, good with figures, good with marketing, good with art, good with computers, good with everything. And they will come to me saying, "This is what makes it so hard. I have a lot of abilities, and I enjoy a lot of things. That makes it hard to choose what to do."

That is a real problem, but most of the time, it is not *the* problem. If that were the real problem, the person would, at some point in time, trade in several good things for something better and be happy with that passion. Or she would even consider two equally good things and pick one, just to get moving. Or she would find, after some searching, some setting in which she can do several things well (the corporate executive training I referred to earlier is a good example). But her desire to get on with life would be greater than her desire to do everything all the time.

If those solutions aren't working, I think that the *real* problem is not the gift of having multiple abilities and multiple passions; rather, it is an issue of being unable to tolerate the loss of options. Life and leadership require that you give up good things and good opportunities in order to carve the best path. It would be easy if the alternatives were horrible: do you want this low-paying dead-end job, or do you want the corner office with the windows? In that scenario, one's passion would be evident!

One aspect of character growth and maturity is the ability to lose the good in order to gain the better. This requires that you learn invaluable skills such as commitment, self-control, patience, adaptation, risk, letting go, sadness, accepting limitations and loss, and going deeper instead of broader. It is how people succeed long term in the game of life.

When one of my sons was a high school senior, he went through that rite of passage called choosing a college. For several months, he researched, interviewed, and toured the campuses of several schools. He enjoyed that part of the process. But when several schools accepted him, it stopped being fun. He felt overwhelmed with the choices. A school with thirty thousand students meant giving up a small, intimate setting. A school that specialized in business meant saying no to one that had a great media arts program. His close friends were all going to different schools, so no matter where he went, he would lose those contacts. One day he told me, "I wish just one school had accepted me; that would have been so much easier." But this is how we grow up. He had to say no to the good, to say yes to the best.

You sometimes see this same problem among singles who are afraid of committing to a long-term relationship. Or some people even have the *no losses* problem in making decisions such as where to live. But don't confuse these problems with having lots of choices or lots of abilities. Begin, instead, to address how awful it feels to say no to good things and walk away from them. Learn to tolerate that, and identifying your passion will come easier.

As poet Robert Frost says:

> Two roads diverged in a yellow wood,
> And sorry I could not travel both
> And be one traveler, long I stood
> And looked down one as far as I could
> To where it bent in the undergrowth.
> Then took the other, as just as fair.[2]

We all have to face—with sorrow—that we will have to choose one path and say good-bye to another. But it is worth it. It is "just as fair." And it is how leaders overcome this obstacle to identifying their passion.

Perfectionism

Perfectionism is similar to the problem of losing options. When you have difficulty with accepting reality and are only okay when you or your situation is ideal, you can be paralyzed in choosing a passion. When the ideal is a demand rather than a goal, the ideal becomes the enemy of the real. Choosing a passion requires choosing something that is not perfect. It may mean taking a job that has problems or marrying someone who has faults. And it may also require being on a learning curve in which you are forced to make lots of mistakes and come to terms with your own imperfections. So perfectionists often procrastinate on committing to their passion. It is less frightening to think of themselves in terms of potentials and a bright future, than it is to jump in the water and face realities about themselves that are not always pleasant. The only solution is letting go of the ideal as a requirement and holding on to it as a goal. Then you can enter reality and accept what truly is, in order to succeed in a world that is real.

This is why the best leaders are never "perfectionistic." They believe in excellence and quality, and they have high standards. But they face the realities about themselves, and about those they lead, with grace and patience. No one can survive a perfectionistic leader for very long without becoming either discouraged or simply tuning out and pretending. As a leader, keep the distinction between excellence and perfection clear—in your own mind and for those who are looking to you.

Respect Your Emotions

I hope that you now feel more equipped and more comfortable in giving your emotions the respect they deserve in leadership. They need to be taken out of the shadows and used as the strong allies they can be in the process of influencing and making changes in your organization. The successful leader leads with reason *and* with feelings.

In part 4, we'll continue to explore emotions, but within the context of how you relate to and connect with others. Your relational world, an essential part of your inner and intuitive world, is a key to being with, understanding, inspiring, and leading others well.

PART IV

RELATIONSHIPS

CONNECTING WITH THOSE YOU LEAD

A close friend of mine, Eric Heard, a pastor who is involved in leadership development, told me a story of how his own leader, Chuck Swindoll, made a lasting impression on him. Chuck was senior pastor of the church Eric worked in for many years, and he was Eric's immediate superior. In addition to being a nationally known pastor, author, and radio teacher, Chuck's work at the time also involved hosting and speaking at cruises for people who listened to his radio program. Eric accompanied Chuck on one of those events. During the cruise, Chuck received word that Eric's father had suddenly died back in the United States. Instead of sending someone else to tell Eric, Chuck dropped everything he was doing to find Eric and tell him personally. It took Chuck more than an hour to locate Eric on the huge ship.

After Chuck told Eric that his father had died, he asked, "Do you want to talk?" Eric said he did, and they walked to the back of the ship and talked for more than an hour. Eric poured out his heart. It was an especially painful time for him because he and his dad had severe conflict that had never been reconciled—and now never would be. Chuck said nothing while Eric talked. No wonderful quotes. No sage advice. No Scriptures.

He listened and allowed Eric to let go. In time, this helped him begin to regain his stability and take the next steps to move on.

This is typical of who Chuck Swindoll is as a man and as a leader. Eric had many similar experiences with him in their years together at the church, though none as profound as this one. Chuck trained Eric for a long time. A few years after their conversation on the ship, both moved on to new settings. But Eric told me that Chuck is one of the few individuals in his life that, if he were to call from anywhere in the world and ask for him, Eric would immediately get on the next plane. Chuck's character, and his relationship with Eric, marked Eric for life. He considers Chuck one of the keys to the successes in his own leadership and career.

Leadership must include competency, skills, and vision, but ultimately it must also go beyond and enter the realm of relationship. It is connectedness that fuels your people to continue with your endeavors. It is the ability to make the connection that keeps them committed to your ideas and objectives. Chuck's impact on Eric was profound, in the same way that other leaders in my life profoundly affected me. You can probably look back and remember one or two people who also took you under their wing for a time of development. It is relationship that glues together all the other skills and tactics of leadership.

This does not mean, however, that you must become someone's counselor or confidante in order to connect relationally. Nor does it mean that you are to lower standards, ignore confrontation, or abandon your drive for results. Those must stay in place. It does mean, however, that you need to add relational abilities to your tool chest of skills when you seek to lead others. The better you understand and use your relational world in your leadership, the better your decisions, plans, and visions will operate.

Chapter 8

RELATIONAL IMAGES

O kay, so how in the world did you pull it off?" I asked Harold, a friend of mine who owns a manufacturing company. Harold had just succeeded in moving his entire organization to a different state in a very short period of time, and he did it on time and under budget. It had taken an enormous amount of planning and energy, and I was in awe of his achievement.

"I get the logistical part," I said, "but how did you stay focused and keep pressing forward?"

"There were times I almost didn't make it," Harold said. "Nights and weekends I was helping my family move and make the adjustments. That was on top of long days at the office. There were times I doubted myself and wondered if I was an idiot for even thinking about this project."

"I get that," I said. "So what kept you going?"

"Coach Williams," he said with a smile. I knew Harold had played college football, and he had previously mentioned his coach.

"You mean you would call him up and ask his advice?"

"No," Harold said. "I mean whenever I was at a low, Coach's face would pop up in my head and I'd remember how many times he would tell me, 'Harold, you are made of the right stuff. I have seen you excel and persist. I believe in you.' When I replayed those memories, I would literally feel energy to keep going. And all I can say is, 'Thanks, Coach Williams.'"

Harold's story demonstrates the power of "relational images." Relational images are significant people whose words or example we internalize in some way. All of us possess these images. They can include people in our present, as well as people in our past. A mental image is more than an intellectual memory, though that is involved. It is somewhat three-dimensional, and more alive, in a sense. When you think about these significant people, you may see their face, remember something they said to you, and draw up the feelings you had or have for each other.

For example, you have relational images of your parents. Think for a minute of your father—if he was involved in your life. Remember how he looked at different ages over the years. Remember some of the favorite (or not-so-favorite) often-repeated phrases he said that you have never forgotten. Remember the feelings you experienced toward him. Some sporting or cultural event or outing you attended with him. There may be some painful or negative parts of that image as well because our relationships with our parents are intense and complex. Your relational images contain many aspects of what happened between you and the people who have mattered most to you. Now, compare that experience to a factual memory of your father, for example, "He was an honest man and he was a hard worker." That is all true, but you don't really "know" the man until a relational image comes into play.

I asked you to reflect on a relational image because I want you to stop for a moment and begin digging into a great well of meaningful people in your life, people who can help you lead better. For most leaders, drawing from a well of relational memories and experiences is a valuable but untapped resource.

Like Harold, you can use this tool to help you persevere in difficult times. Your relational images can provide strategic clarity, creative vision, and empathic people skills when you need them most.

The Benefits of Relational Images

To use a banking analogy, relational images are like an internal investment account. This account corresponds to a person who has been important to you. Over the course of your relationship with that individual, you make deposits into that account. You deposit memories, thoughts, mental pictures, and emotions. You do it all the time without knowing it. Your mind just does it for you. Psychologists call the process of making those deposits *internalization*. You are literally "taking in" your experience of that person. And the account forms an integrated picture, or representation, of that person as you have known him or her.

We know a great deal about how we develop relational images by observing infant and child development. As newborns, one of our first tasks in life is to create and internalize pictures of our parents, in order to become safe, confident, and calm. This process continues throughout our lives. And it's why I used the analogy of an investment account. Positive, healthy relational images—emotional memories of supportive, helpful people in your life—always pay dividends. These images continue helping us to be the best we can be, even when the actual person is no longer present. Without relational images, we would not be able to function well in life. Things you take for granted, such as the ability to make connections with others, to be courageous enough to take risks, to have self-confidence, and to confront problems, would not work as well if you did not have good relational images to draw on. Though you may not be aware of them, they are always operating in the background. They help you to do things like focus under pressure and create new opportunities for yourself.

However, it's important to note that not all relational images are positive, and negative relational images do not pay fruitful dividends. You can be debilitated by images that are defeating and judgmental. A client of mine who was CFO of a large company struggled with paralyzing self-doubt when he had to make a complicated financial decision. We traced it to a relational image of a mother who repeatedly said things like, "You can't let the family down. Don't embarrass us. You're a Smith."

You internalize anyone who is significant to you, past and present. And the people you lead are internalizing *you*. In order to be an effective leader, you need to take this fact seriously. To a large extent, the mental and emotional pictures people have of you—based on how you relate to and lead them—is up to you.

There are many ways you can use your healthy relational images to strengthen your leadership. As we focus in on five key benefits, consider how each one might apply to a leadership issue or challenge you're facing right now.

Benefit 1: Drawing Strength and Support under Stress

When you have a conflict with someone at work or when you are under lots of pressure, you need strength and support. Sooner or later, you need some form of help that comes from the outside. Willpower, commitment, and determination can certainly help you push through difficult times, but they aren't enough to keep you going when things are bad.

Relationships are the fuel you need to be calm, confident, and to keep going during tough times. Sometimes it might mean a two-minute phone call just to tell a friend that things are difficult right now. Or it may be taking the opportunity to have lunch with someone and discuss your situation. But there are also those times when a serious problem hits and you are truly alone. In those times, you must draw on your relational images. That is what they are for. They are meant to sustain you when you are hit hard.

I was in a small support group with Ross, a businessman who was having a problem at work. One of his direct reports was apparently after his job and was using unethical tactics to bring him down. The direct report was spreading rumors about Ross and, as it happened, some people believed them. Individuals were taking sides, and the conflict was coming to a destructive head. In the small group, we spent a lot of time listening to Ross, encouraging him, and being there for him. There wasn't a lot of advice we could give, as he had already told us his next steps. But we wanted him to know we were on his side, whatever happened.

Ross arranged a meeting with the CEO, with his direct report there, to hash it out, face to face. Ross was not a confrontational type, so he was dreading this meeting. But he was resolute and knew it had to go this way.

The day the meeting was scheduled, I got a call from Ross late in the afternoon. I asked how it went. "Really, really tough," he said. "The guy lied through his teeth and totally blew up at me a couple of times."

"That sounds brutal," I said. "How did it end up?"

"Actually, things ended up okay. The CEO saw through his tactics and called it on my side. I think the guy is gone."

"Congratulations!" I said. "You hung in there."

Ross was quiet for a second, and then said, "You want to know what was weird? Right in the thick of it, when the guy was going crazy on me, and I was sitting there, having to take it, do you know what I thought of?"

"What?"

"You guys in the group. Your faces just came up on the screen in my head, while he was calling me every name in the book. I saw you being on my side, believing in me, and being my friends. I knew I wasn't all by myself. I don't know how it happened, but I'll tell you, you guys were there with me in that room, and you kept me sane during the meeting."

Ross's experience is an example of what we can all do when we're up against a difficult situation. Leaders encounter enormous stresses from many directions. When times are tough, access your relational images and make a withdrawal. They will see you through.

So how can you make this actionable in your leadership? First, *be intentional in identifying and collecting these relational experiences.* Make the investments in yourself. The disconnected workaholic leader risks a deficit in great, healthy relational images. Get around the right people, and ask for their support. Second, *resist the temptation to draw on "you," and instead draw on "them."* I have no patience for personal growth books that effectively say, "You have everything you need inside, just tap into it." To begin with, it's not true. We need God, and we are to look up and call out to him for help: "Call to me," God says through the prophet Jeremiah, "and I will answer you and tell you great and unsearchable things you do not know" (Jeremiah 33:3). No amount of navel-gazing can access that kind of help. I have also worked with too many leaders whose only tool was to tell themselves, "Work harder, push through." While that can sometimes be helpful, it does not help nearly as much as utilizing the support, grace, and truth of those who have "been there" with you. The wisdom writer puts it this way: "Pity anyone who falls and has no one to help them up" (Ecclesiastes 4:10).

It's also important to keep in mind the power of the relational images your leadership creates in those you lead. I got a good reminder of this when I recently ran into a former employee I hadn't seen for several years. We were catching up, and he said, "You changed my life with what you said." I had no clue what he was talking about. "I'm glad," I told him, "but what was it I said?"

"We were just riding down in the elevator one day," he said, "and you mentioned I had some unique people skills and strengths and suggested that I consider developing them. I thought about that conversation so many times afterward, and I realized I wanted to become a therapist. I went back to school, got my degree, and now I have my own practice. It's where I was meant to be."

I vaguely remembered our conversation, but note that he remembered even the location where it took place. That's just one example of the power your words and example can have, even in seemingly insignificant moments like an elevator ride.

Benefit 2: Becoming a Relationally Based Person

Warm and stable relational images help you to become a more relational person. While leaders must be highly task-based, they need also to be relational in order to keep people around them. Having healthy relational images forms the belief in you that relationship is the best place in the world to be. Life is essentially about relationships, and it is empty without relationships. This is especially true with the leader.

For leaders, being with people—giving and receiving—is a primary and important focus. You draw on your relational images when you are alone, you use them to gain support and strength, and you carry on. Then, when you are around the real flesh-and-blood people in your life, you gain support and strength from them. In the process, you make even more deposits into your relational images account, internalizing this truth: *Because these images are good for me, relationship is good for me.* It helps you to become a relationship-seeking person. Now you are drawing on two sources: the images and the real thing.

When I speak at leaders' conferences about successful relationships, I often talk about how leaders need to be not only givers of encouragement, but also receivers. It's been my experience that leaders aren't very good at taking in support from others. They provide it, but they end up getting drained themselves. So I ask them who they go to for their own strength and support. And I remind them, "Your spouse and your dog aren't enough."

The spouses of the leaders in the audience often come up to me afterward and say, "Thanks for saying the part about me and the dog." Spouses get drained from being the only emotional support system the leader has. You need to take undue pressure off your spouse and get a few good friends who are safe and understand you. Spend regular time with them; maybe start a weekly group. There are many ways this can happen.

If your only close friend is your spouse, you may be in jeopardy of turning him or her into your parent. And that is a bad recipe for a marriage. Sometimes I will give a leader this homework assignment: Ask your spouse, "Would you be happier if I had other close friends to talk to besides you?" See what your spouse says. Broaden your relational contact, and get several people around you. That is the beginning of becoming a relationally based person. There's no place better to be than in relationship.

As a leader, you also have a responsibility to make sure the members of your team have what they need to perform at their best. That's why it's important for you to encourage them to become relationally based with people in their lives as well, to fuel them so they are up to the challenges they face.

Benefit 3: Having a Source of Wisdom and Guidance

The good people you have internalized, and are still internalizing, are a tremendous resource of direction, encouragement, and information for you. When you are tempted to take a short cut, avoid a complex situation, or don't have a good answer for a problem, your relational images can remind you of your values, of what is truly important. That is the essence of the mentoring and coaching process. You internalize hours of wisdom from your coach. You practice the concepts you are learning. And eventually, you have done enough work with that person that, in a given situation, you know what your coach would likely say to you— even if he or she has never said it. In other words, you haven't simply remembered a list of principles. You have internalized the way your coach thinks and responds.

A friend of mine has had a leadership coach for a while, and their relationship has brought positive results to his work and leadership. He recently told me a story about how he is more focused and more effective with people as a result of meeting with his coach. He had to move an individual at work to another position because she wasn't working out where she was. However, he knew she wanted to stay in her current position and could be very manipulative and reactive. On top of that, he had a weakness in feeling guilty when someone resisted his decisions, so he was not looking forward to the meeting. But he and his coach were working on that issue. I knew his coach, and I knew that though he was a kind person, he could also be very direct. He didn't suffer fools gladly.

After the meeting, my friend told me that the employee had been predictably tough to deal with. She had cried, claimed he was being unfair, and said she was doing her best. It really tugged at his guilt strings. He listened and reasoned, listened and reasoned. He went above and beyond the call. And he had been tempted to give in and say, "Okay, I'll find another way to make it work where you are." That would have been the easy thing to do.

But while he was listening to her, he imagined his coach looking at her and saying, "I've listened to your reasons, and I have thought about it a lot. I've made my decision and it's final. I just wanted you to know." And then he saw the coach standing up, looking at the woman until she stood up, and walking her to the door of the office, seeing her out, and shutting the door. My friend had never actually seen the coach do that; the coach didn't know the woman. But *he knew the coach*. He knew the coach was the kind of person who could and would do that. And when he thought that, my friend put his thoughts into actions. He kindly but firmly told his employee that the decision was final, stood up, and saw her out. He accomplished a task that was very difficult for him. The deposit his coach had made was more than words. It was an aspect of wisdom and guidance that my friend had internalized and had been able to use.

Using your relational images does not always involve seeing or remembering someone. It's not like Obi Wan Kenobi suddenly appearing in a hologram and saying, "Use the force, Luke." Although that tends to happen early in the internalization stage, what happens over time is that the more you use your relational images, the more they transform into a part of you. That is, they are no longer what you would see the coach doing. Standing up and walking the person out becomes a normal and automatic part of what you do. Over time, your relational images form a part of your own character, identity, and inner life.

When you are faced with a challenge, make it a habit to go through your internal database and search for a relational image of a person who has done well in that arena or has affirmed you in previous challenges. It might be someone like Coach Williams or it might be someone like my friend's mentor who sees a disgruntled employee out the door. Whomever it is, you may be surprised at how helpful those memories can be for you.

As a leader, talk to your directs about this as well. When discussing their challenges, ask them who comes to mind when they think about someone who has been supportive or demonstrated wisdom in similar circumstances. Just don't let them always say, "It's you, boss!"

Benefit 4: Discerning Character in Others

If you have ever hired the wrong person, trusted the wrong person, or invested in the wrong person, you know the importance of being able to discern character in people. The people you spend time with are the people who will influence your life and work, for good or for bad. They can literally make you or break you. As the apostle Paul says, "Bad company corrupts good character" (1 Corinthians 15:33). It can end up costing you sleep, money, energy, and success.

Many of us prefer to give people a break and overlook an offense. That is just being kind, and it is how we want to be treated. However, some individuals have serious character flaws that need to be dealt with. They may be gifted and positive people, but they can have established patterns of irresponsibility, deceit, narcissism, or control that can cause damage to you, your vision, and your organization. They aren't hopeless cases if they want to change, but until they *want* to change, there isn't much hope for them. I have seen many people with character flaws who chose to address them and made permanent changes. However, there are also times when a character flaw might be so severe, coupled with a lack of motivation to own the problem and work on it, that your group isn't the right fit for them—nor them for you.[1]

Many leaders don't automatically know how to discern character in others, how to pick out the good guys from the bad guys. If you are not a naturally intuitive person about these kinds of things, then one of the best sources to help you develop that skill is your relational images. These images help form a template for *good* relationships, if you have good and healthy ones. The better quality of people you have had in your life, the better your ability to identify new high-quality people. This is an invaluable ability, especially if part of what you do is interview, hire, and recommend people for placement or promotion in your organization.

You can compare and contrast new people in your life against the backdrop of your relational images. Responsible, honest, and caring people will compare well. As you talk to them, you will say to yourself, *This person is familiar; he or she reminds me of the good people I've known.* Or it could be that you receive a mental alert: *Something is wrong here.* You've compared that person to your relational images. In this sense, your relational images and your intuition intersect.

It's like the story of how banks train new tellers to identify counterfeit paper currency. For weeks, they allow them to touch only real bills. So, for an intense training time, the tellers handle thousands and thousands of dollars of authentic money. Because they have become so familiar with authentic bills, when they encounter counterfeit money, something doesn't feel right. The alert goes off in their heads because they have had so much experience with the real thing. In the same way, when you internalize the qualities of people who have good character, you can quickly spot those who don't.

As I mentioned earlier, during the past several years, Dr. Henry Cloud and I have conducted a weeklong training experience for leaders called the Ultimate Leadership Workshop. We have several of these every year at a Southern California retreat setting. When I teach at these workshops, I often ask the group, "Who is the last person you chose for your work or your life who wasn't the right person? What trait about that person did you overlook, and why?" After a few seconds of reflection, people will groan and say something like:

- "I overlooked an inability to receive feedback because he had the right skill set."

- "I overlooked a bad work ethic because she stroked my ego."
- "I overlooked an insensitive bedside manner because she was a go-getter."
- "I overlooked deceit because everyone liked his personality."

This is where many lights come on. It's not that they chose people who had solid character and then somehow, overnight and out of the blue, became troublemakers. People with character issues usually have had them for a long time. The reality is that these leaders failed to discern bad things about these people because they were so focused on the good things they wanted. You cannot blame leaders for desiring a good package; that is important. But they minimized or disregarded the negative, in hopes that the positive would net it out in their favor. And, invariably, in the work these leaders did at the workshop, they would unpack their own relational images and find why they minimized the importance of serious flaws. A parent who was emotionally absent or cold. A long-term relationship that flattered but did not have substance. In other words, the leaders' relational images were of dysfunctional people and thus distorted their judgment. Then, as these leaders became more aware of their negative relational images, they were better equipped to connect with healthier people and form better relational images.

One way to make this practical is to start by writing a simple list of the top three times in the last year that you put up with bad attitudes or behavior with a direct report, a client, or someone else at work. For each item on the list, answer the question I posed to the workshop attendees: *What trait about that person did you overlook, and why?* Promise yourself to be vigilant in paying attention to this tendency in yourself, and to not let yourself be hijacked again. Awareness brings behavioral change.

Benefit 5: Giving to Those You Lead

Leadership has to do with relationship. And relationship means that you, the leader, need to be able to understand and give to those you lead. You aren't their spouse, parent, or support group. But you matter to them. You affect them. They are internalizing you. So if you want people to try their best for you, they must know that you want their best as well.

Relational images supply you with two things: the compassion to give to others and the ability to understand others. One is a motivation from the inner world. The other is a skill. Compassion is a motivation that comes out of your gratitude for what you have received. You want to return the favor, to give understanding to other people. The ability to understand comes from observing how you have been understood. If you have been valued, cared about, and trained by significant people in your life, those experiences have been deposited in your relational images investment account. They are there for you to draw on and know how to give as you have been given to.

Let's return to Eric, whose story I told at the beginning of this chapter. He is a very successful leader whose life has transformed the lives of many people for years. He gives to those he leads. He is compassionate, and he understands. He will tell you that much of the compassion comes from his many experiences with Chuck Swindoll, and he is grateful for someone who cared enough not only to sit with him at a time he was in crisis, but to also mentor and guide him through the everyday and routine tasks of leadership. And he will tell you that his ability to listen and understand those he is leading has much to do with how he was listened to.

Building Up Good Relational Images

You may be realizing that you don't have the quality relational-images investment portfolio you would like to have. It is common for one or several of our relational images to be unhealthy. Some of your own significant relationships may have been with people who were cold, controlling, manipulative, self-centered, critical, or even abusive. This can create distorted or nonfunctioning pictures of how relationships should work. Like the leaders in the workshop who realized why they picked the wrong people, you may have drawn on relational images that didn't help you. Or you may simply have rejected all images, not trusting them, and decided to go it on your own instead. In these instances, you may be able to operate successfully for a while by drawing on your best judgment and your best skills. However, your judgment and skills are a limited resource—they will not be enough to sustain you for long-term leadership. If you recognize that your relational images portfolio isn't what it should be, the best thing you can do is to be intentional about making some new investments—developing good and healthy relational images.

The principle is simple: *Take in the good and forgive and grow from the bad.* You will need, today, in the present, to be intentional about finding the right people to start a new relational investment portfolio, so to speak. You are never too old to internalize good relational images. Look around your context and latch on to the good people. Find a coach or mentor who has a good reputation in the community. Get involved in a small group. Seek out a good therapist who understands leadership dynamics.

The more regularly you meet with the good people and the more vulnerable and open you are with them, the better the return you'll get from your relational images investments. In this way, you become emotionally present—that is, you are in touch with and talk about your feelings as well as your thoughts. Open your life, your dreams, your struggles—your inner world—to the right people. Let them in so they can provide you with the good elements we've discussed: strength and support, wisdom and guidance, and all the rest.

The negative relational images you will need to forgive. Forgiveness is a wonderful way out of mental, emotional, and spiritual prison. It lets you give up the demand for justice, allows you to be free of another person's harm, and helps you heal and move on from the past. Forgiveness is a way of outgrowing whatever happened in those tough relationships, to understand the pain, to learn the right lessons, and to be a bigger person. The combination of taking in the good and forgiving the bad will help you to become a fundamentally better person as well as a more effective leader.[2]

Next Steps

When I give talks about relational images, I sometimes get pushback or questions about the practicality of using them in leadership. People will sometimes say things like, "This sounds like vague psychobabble stuff rather than leadership stuff." I may be a shrink, but this content is not vague psychobabble, and I can assure you that once you get the hang of it, you will find that using your relational images is very helpful. Here are three ways you can begin to make this practical in your everyday work and leadership.

- Make a list of the five most helpful or influential people in your life, people who have helped you become the person you are or to achieve what you've achieved. Write down a few examples of what they said or did that influenced you, and what you felt or experienced when you heard or witnessed these impactful things. Refer back to this list when you are facing a challenge and need wisdom or encouragement.
- Write a one- or two-paragraph summary of a financial, operational, or cultural challenge you're facing in your organization. Then identify someone who believed in you and has been successful, and imagine how they might respond to what you've written. Write another paragraph or two in that person's voice. What do you imagine this person might say to help you over the hurdle?
- Be specific and intentional about the relational image you want to invest in your direct reports and others with whom you work. Start with your one-on-one meetings. Before you meet with each person, briefly reflect on what you think he or she needs to hear from you, such as encouragement, guidance, correction, challenge, etc. During the meeting, eliminate distractions and focus on that person with 100 percent eye contact. Be as emotionally present as possible, and model what it looks like to give full attention to someone. After the meeting, evaluate how well you provided your direct reports with the appropriate relational image of a leader he or she needed at that time.

In addition to building up a portfolio of positive relational images for yourself and your team, there is an additional set of relational skills that are just as critical for your leadership. In order to lead effectively, it is essential to practice and strengthen seven specific abilities in how you relate to those you lead, which is what the next chapter is all about.

Chapter 9

RELATIONAL ABILITIES

One way to quickly assess the importance of a leadership skill or ability is to consider the potential consequences when that skill or ability is absent. So what happens when leaders lack relational abilities? Consider the following nightmare scenarios, some of which you may be able to relate to:

- The CEO of a nonprofit organization has a habit of answering every concern of his volunteers with statements like, "I'm sure it's not that bad; you'll do fine." With those empty pats on the back, the volunteers become demoralized and many quit.
- A workaholic physician who is a part owner in a medical practice becomes frustrated with her office staff because they don't live by the same dictum she does: "FILO: *first in* the office, *last out* of the office." She makes it clear that she's disappointed in what she considers their lack of commitment. They just try to avoid her.
- The chair of a university physics department is highly conflict avoidant. When one of his faculty members gets consistently poor student evaluation ratings because of lack of planning and structure, he puts off having the tough conversation required to address the issue. The other faculty members notice, and are discouraged.

No matter how gifted each of these leaders may be or how hard they work, a lack of relational ability undermines their efforts to lead effectively and achieve their objectives. In fact, there is a flood of recent research demonstrating that how leaders relate is a critical factor in how well they perform. For example, the firm Talent Smart has concluded that over 90 percent of top performing leaders have high EQ, the well-known trait of emotional intelligence.

Relational abilities help you effectively channel your managing, training, and problem-solving with people because you are able to work well with them. And the good news is that relational abilities are skills you can learn and develop.

Seven Relational Abilities Every Leader Needs

I am an obsessive observational note-taker, especially when I work with leaders. After every consultation, I write up my observations about how I see them behaving and relating with others. This gives me a great deal of data to draw on when I need to identify the strengths they need to build on, and the changes they need to make to improve on any weaknesses. An additional benefit is that, over the years, I have observed an emerging pattern, a consistent set of relational abilities among the best and most effective leaders. On the pages that follow, we'll explore these seven traits, and consider practical ways you can develop these skills and use them to help your people maximize their own potential in the organization.

1. Empathy

Empathy is the ability to put your own experience on the back burner and enter into the experience of another person. It is not mind reading, and it is not sympathy. It is being able to walk in that person's shoes, to see work and people and life from the other person's perspective. Far from being valuable only in understanding people's emotional pain, empathy is extremely useful in leadership settings. When you are able to empathize with those you lead, two good things happen. First, you are better able to develop and assist them because you know what's going on. Second, they are more willing for you to lead them because they experience the empathy as an indication that you understand and are there for them.

During the time I was on the board of a charity organization, the board chair invited someone new to join. She asked this man because he was good with finances, an ability the board needed to have. He came to a meeting so we could all get to know one another.

It quickly became apparent that this man was extremely uncomfortable with the rest of us. He seemed very anxious, couldn't get his words out right, and corrected himself over and over. I felt really sorry for his discomfort. From what I found out afterward, the problem was that he felt intimidated by the board. He was younger than the rest of us, was fairly new in his profession, and had just relocated from another part of the country. So apparently he felt he didn't belong.

It wasn't going well, but we were all plugging along in the meeting. Then the board chair said these words: "Bill, I am sure this is not easy for you. If I were in your position, I would be very uncomfortable too. But I want you to know that you are here because you have already proven yourself in other places. We really do respect and value what you bring to us."

It was like a spell had been broken. Bill thanked her, and you could see his shoulders lift and his confidence return. He started relating with us like just one of the crew, and the rest of the meeting, along with the subsequent ones, went fine after that. The board chair provided empathy and then respect. But the empathy had to come first before he could hear the respect.

I often see leaders confusing empathy with being positive. They think they are offering empathy by being supportive, encouraging, and hopeful. But in the process, they don't really listen to the bad news, such as discouragement, failure, or fear. Most of them think that going there with the bad news might send those they lead into a black hole of despair, so they focus on cheering their people back up to happiness. The problem is that relationships don't work that way. When you are understood and receive empathy for a bad time, it actually encourages you because you feel less alone with the bad experience. It is the compassionate presence more than the upbeat words of another person that bring hope and cheer. When you know you aren't alone, you can bear just about anything. It is the sense of isolation that keeps a bad feeling bad.

So when *cheery* leaders don't empathize with their people well, they actually compound the problem they are trying to solve. By not hearing the bad news, they are further isolating the person's struggle, and the individual feels even more alone, thinking, *Here I am, discouraged, and my leader wants me to look at the bright side.* The result is usually that the person feels guilty and more of a failure for not being "up" enough to please the boss, or just disconnects from the leader and shuts down while nodding his or her head in some sort of external show of compliance. Neither of these are good outcomes. So don't be afraid to truly empathize. It leads to hope.

Here are a few simple but practical ways to practice empathy:

- Move toward the person's discomfort rather than trying to move them away from their discomfort. Authentically use statements such as, "That's got to be tough/overwhelming/discouraging," to convey you are *with them* in the hardship, not that you are trying to get them to change their perspective.
- Match your body language, verbal tone, and eye contact to theirs, which is likely quiet and more serious rather than sparky and cheery.
- Briefly restate what you heard them say, and then ask if you're understanding them accurately. For example, "Is that what you feel?" "Is that what it's like for you?" "Am I getting that right?"

I was working with a client on her empathy skills, and she said, "I get that this helps them trust me, but it seems a bit unproductive not to give them advice."

"Absolutely," I said, "empathy creates openness in them so they can hear and metabolize your advice. Give lots of solutions, but always begin with empathy."

You don't have to do this every time someone has a challenge. For example, "I dropped my pen," doesn't require, "Wow, that must be awful." But when something matters to the person, it should matter enough to you to be empathetic.

Examples of Non-Empathetic and Empathetic Responses

Scenario	Non-Empathetic Response	Empathetic Response
A direct report expresses discouragement about a second failed attempt to increase sales of a new product or service.	"Go for it, you'll get there. You've got what it takes!"	"I know how hard you've been working on this second attempt, and it's got to be disheartening for you. Let's talk about what happened this time and find a solution."
A volunteer is thinking of quitting because of relational challenges with another volunteer.	"Just be patient with him. People grow and change over time."	"I'm sure this isn't easy. I know you've been trying hard to connect with him. I don't want you to leave, so let's brainstorm some options."
A colleague acknowledges fears about doing a good job on an upcoming presentation.	"Suck it up, buttercup, life's not easy. Besides, you always do a great job."	"I totally get it. I've been paralyzed myself in this situation. Want to run through it with me and I'll give you some feedback?"
A small group member admits to feeling like she will never overcome her struggles with an addiction.	"Are you sure you're really surrendered to God, like 100 percent surrendered?"	"That sounds hard and overwhelming. As a group, let's focus on the most disruptive issue you're facing right now and see if we can help."

2. Relational Independence

An important relational ability for you as a leader is to see people as separate from you and from their roles with you. Your people want to work with you, or they wouldn't be with you. But you aren't their reason for existing. They have lives, dreams, and concerns of their own. You need to be able to identify and understand that. Sometimes leaders assume everyone has the organizational vision as strongly as they do or are as committed as they are. That can be a mistake and can undo what you are trying to accomplish with your team.

Did you ever watch *The Office,* the TV "mockumentary" about the everyday lives of office employees in a paper company? The lead character, Michael Scott, is one of the worst managers imaginable. One of his typical gaffes is how he introduces new ideas. He walks into the common area where all of the employees are busy taking phone orders, working with accounts, and doing financial analyses. In a loud voice, he pronounces his new idea to everyone, thinking that they will naturally be as on fire for it as he is. As he eagerly anticipates their enthusiastic response, the camera then pans over the faces of the staff, all of whom are looking at him silently, waiting for him to go away so they can get back to their jobs. He is usually either disappointed in their underwhelming reaction, or he is clueless and continues on, oblivious to their disconnection from him. Michael is not aware that his people are separate from him.

Inspiring your team is as important as building commitment and cultivating shared values. But always keep in mind that before you walk in the room, people are probably thinking about their own lives and their own parts of the job. Respect that, and work with that. You want them to know that they matter more to you than simply what they can do for you. They aren't merely an extension of your vision. Ironically, if you convey this sort of respect, you generally receive more commitment from those you lead because they feel safer with you.

Here is a helpful skill to execute this ability, in a stepwise fashion:

- Write down three things that motivate and energize you in your job. It may be something like achieving your mission, making a difference, or being with great people.
- Then, for each person on your team, write down three things you think motivate and energize them—but don't assume their motivations are the same as yours. For example, they may be motivated by problem solving, compensation, or flexible hours.

- Without telling them what you wrote in your own musings, ask each person for their top three motivators. In this way, you will not only see how well you understand their experience, but also how to appreciate and motivate them based on what truly matters most to them.

3. Relationship and Reality

As a leader, you are to provide reality for your people in the form of training, management, guidance, structure, advice, recommendations, feedback, and confrontation. I define reality for the leader as *what is true, whether positive or negative*. Reality might mean that the team crushed a goal, and it's time to celebrate. Or it might mean that the wheels fell off of an initiative, and it's time to learn what went wrong. You give your people the information, truths, and experiences they lack or have lost sight of. Whether you facilitate a small group, lead a team of vice presidents, employ several workers, or run a volunteer organization, you are the provider of the realities they need in order to resource and accomplish their tasks.

Successful leaders learn to provide relationship and reality at the same time. In other words, they develop relational connection so their people can more effectively receive and use the reality. Relationship provides the bridge over which truth can be conveyed.

In your leadership, your people will experience truth in the absence of relationship as harshness, judgment, or condemnation. They will resist and refuse it, either actively or subtly. Truth is hard to swallow if you don't feel connected with the truth teller. That is why being "for" the other person, letting them know that, and being as emotionally accessible as possible *at the time of the reality*, is critical.

A client of mine had what might be called a poor bedside manner with her direct reports. When they screwed up, she instantly went to correction mode. She wasn't trying to be harsh, she was actually trying to solve the problem. It was a simple case of relational cluelessness.

She reported to me that her sales manager had been defensive when she tried to talk with him about a low-performance month, and said, "All I need is for him to admit he was part of it instead of blaming his salespeople. But he keeps saying he didn't do anything wrong."

Knowing her, I said, "Try this. Go to him again, and paraphrase his own experience. From what you've told me, that would be something like, 'I can imagine it's been frustrating to spend all your time and bandwidth on the team this month, and to still have discouraging results. Let's talk about some things I can do better to resource you.'"

"What good will that do?" she asked.

"Hold on a minute," I said, "I'm not done. Once you offer to help, see if he softens up a bit because he can tell you are trying to relate to him. Then ask him, 'If I work on helping you help the team, and if I work resourcing you, is there anything you can do to improve things as well?' I think adding a bit of relationship to reality will help."

She called me the next day. "It worked!" she said. "He admitted he wasn't clear with his people, and they didn't know his priorities."

Here is my point. It probably took her an extra two minutes of relational investment, and it was more than worth it.

Leaders sometimes make a couple of mistakes along this line. The first is that they divide relationship and reality and then alternate them. That is, the relational times are positive, encouraging, and enjoyable—but there is no conveying of the truth. The "truth talk," then, tends to be disconnected and cold. This is generally because the leader is uncomfortable with having both relationship and reality at the same time. She may feel that she can't be direct if she is too warm; she is concerned that she will soften the feedback too much, so she withdraws and becomes businesslike and detached. It's disconcerting for people. They wonder if the leader has a split personality. The solution in these situations is generally to take a few risks and practice being both attuned and truthful at the same time, and see what happens. Most of the time, when a leader attempts to balance relationship and reality, she finds that she doesn't have to back off from the truth to still be a compassionate human being, and people don't mind it.

The other mistake comes from a different direction. Some leaders are very empathic and can attune well to how their people are doing, but they have difficulty providing structure, direction, or feedback when it is necessary. So they end up listening, caring, and understanding but never getting to the point that there is some action step or ownership they provide for the other person. While there are times when empathy is all someone needs, as with the board chair's comment to the new board member who felt uncomfortable, there are also many other times when more is needed.

Leaders who go in this direction aren't overly empathic. I don't believe it's possible to overly care about someone. Rather, such leaders are not truthful enough. They usually perceive those they lead as more fragile than they actually are and don't want to hurt them. It is often helpful for leaders to think about how they, themselves, respond to reality. It doesn't crush or devastate them. It isn't pleasant, but it is tolerable and helpful. In that way, they are often able to keep both elements in place with those they lead.

When communicating reality requires confrontation, it's important to follow the right sequence. Keep the relational aspect first and reality second. It makes the medicine go down easier. That is why, when you need to confront a problem in performance or attitude, you must make sure that the person you are leading knows you are "for" her—that is, on her side—before you proceed.

In an established relationship, where you and the person you lead know each other well, you may not need to actually say anything to make sure things are okay between you and them and that you value them. It's a little like a solid and safe marriage, where you are bugged by something and you just blurt out, "I just saw the credit card statement. Your spending is a problem, and I need to fix this with you!" In safe relationships, the safety is already in position, and you can go ahead and talk about the issue.

However, if it is a new hire, or a person who is unfamiliar with you, it's wise to make sure the person knows you are on her side. Say things that convey value, support, and appreciation—and really mean them. For example: "Lauren, I wanted to meet with you about the quotas, but first I want you to know that I really do value having you on the team. You're a real asset to all of us. But we need to solve this . . ."

There are some people who are defensive or cast blame about everything. No matter what you do, they feel judged, persecuted, or mistreated by even small corrections. If this is the case with the person you're confronting, you need to prepare to deal with that as well. One option is to address that attitude as an issue in itself; help the person see that it exists and that he or she needs to overcome it.[1]

Once you are at the point of giving the hard reality feedback, be clear and direct. That is a great kindness, and it is a very relational thing to do. State the problem, share examples of the problem, describe the ramifications, and suggest the cure you've identified. In that way, you give them a path, something to do about it, and hope.

I once was consulting with an organization in which, after analyzing the issues, I had to give some bad news to one of the leaders. He was a competent person, but he had a pattern of being politically manipulative—that is, using people against each other in order to get some result he wanted. So he had caused some division in the organization, and it was hurting the company. It was a serious situation. His board had tried to talk to him, but he had shut them down and dismissed them as not understanding him. As a neutral consultant, it was decided maybe he would listen to me.

We met, and after the preliminary greeting and small talk, I told him that I thought he was dividing people and manipulating them. He said in an offended tone, "Let me get this straight. Are you saying that I'm being deceitful?"

I thought about how to respond. I considered saying, "That's too strong a word," or "Maybe not on purpose," or "In a way, we all do that." Then I thought, *Just do this.* And I said, "Yes." And I sat there.

He looked at me for a few seconds without saying anything. I suppressed my strong urge to fill up the silent office with explanatory words that would soften things up. I hoped that the silence would, instead, perhaps give him some room to face himself. There was also the possibility I was just giving him more time to figure out ways to manipulate me.

Finally, he sighed and said simply, "You're right. I am."

A lot happened after that, but that was the turning point for him. He became more aware of his manipulative tendencies and more open to feedback from others. We set up a program for him, consisting of a series of accountable relationships with people who would help and support him. It wasn't an overnight success, for the patterns were deeply entrenched. But he worked hard, and he was valuable enough to the company that they stood by him in the process. Ultimately, the process worked for him and for the organization.

This is an example of how helpful a simple and direct declaration of reality can be with those you lead. It clears the air and, as long as there is no judgment or condemnation in your stance and tone, can do the necessary surgery that provides hope for changes and, ultimately, productivity.

4. Motivation

Every leader is concerned about how to motivate those she leads. It's hard to imagine a leader who is not involved, at some level, in influencing others to engage in the mission, see their part, and perform at high levels in the organization. There have been countless ways devised over the years to motivate teams and groups, including financial and benefits incentives, fitting the person to the task, providing a warm environment, resourcing, setting an example, praising, giving feedback, and inspiring.

Motivation is a highly researched and studied area because of its importance in successful leadership. It is certainly a relational ability, as the better you can relate, the better you will be able to influence and motivate. Clearly, motivation involves intuitive abilities—abilities that include relationship.

To increase motivation among your people, create an environment for passion. In other words, sprinkle into your conversations (about roles, goals, and strategy, etc.) with questions such as, "What excites you about what you do here?" or "What would you love to be engaged in here if there were an opportunity?" When your people have a passion for what they do, it may not be the only necessary element of motivation, but it is one of the most important. People will work hard and achieve great results when they have passion for the task.

We explored discovering your own passion in chapter 7. I described it as being an intersection between who you really are, the internal real self, and what you are involved in, the external context. Passion is ignited when the real self connects with the right task environment. It is how we are made.

What works for you also works for those you lead. You can't create passion, not for yourself or for anyone else. However, as a leader, you can create the right environment for the chemistry to happen. You do this by personal research. You must spend the energy to know your people and learn which tasks intersect with their passions. It will be different for different individuals; it's not a one-style-fits-all program. But when you develop this relational ability, and get to know the insides of your people, the value and benefits are enormous.

Here is an example. A friend of mine runs a small business in the service industry. One of his human resources staff members was reasonably competent and handled HR issues well. There were no sparks, but there were no complaints. My friend, however, noticed that this man seemed to be the curious type. He asked questions of the boss about how the company worked, and, more importantly, he asked questions of people in other departments. He was curious about accounting, marketing, sales, and financial services. He did his HR job, but it was clear he had other interests.

Finally, my friend figured out that this man was a "MacGyver," from the 1980s TV show, in which the main character could invent any sort of gadget out of string and gum. In other words, he loved doing a lot of things, and he was good at them. On top of that, he was a better problem-solver than a maintainer. My friend, the boss, understood this, and also knew that, at that period in the company's growth, he needed someone who could be called in interdepartmentally to handle some issue that had come up. Also, that person could give him the street view of what was going on in the company. He created a new position for this man, and it worked very well. People appreciated the extra resource. The return on investment was very high for the company. And MacGyver had a genuine passion for what he did. He was good at it, he had energy for it, and he helped the organization with it.

The MacGyver position may not last forever, as the needs of companies change over time. But the point is, always be on the alert to see what your people love, and if there is a fit somewhere which will create good results for the company and for the person.

Another highly effective tactic to increase motivation is simply *noticing and affirming.* Our brains are wired so that when someone who matters to us notices that we did a great job on a project, or that we have really been reaching out to the team, it's like an instant antidepressant. We simply become motivated to do better after that short conversation. I have been so saddened by employees or volunteers in an organization telling me in private that the only attention they receive is negative attention when there's a problem. Don't be that leader.

5. Freedom and Ownership

The more autonomy and personal accountability people can handle, the more they are motivated. Independence provides your people with the ability to take on ownership for their performance and for the team's productivity. You need to determine the degree of freedom for your contexts.

Some people need little hands-on management from you. They tend to not only value their autonomy, but they have earned the right to it. They are self-structured and bring in results because of their own abilities. I have a friend in the financial services industry who is in sales on a national level. He is the rainmaker for the accounts and secures them. He doesn't manage a large department. Instead, the company built a small team around him to resource him and then to follow up on the accounts after he has landed them. His boss is a relationally perceptive person and understood my friend's wiring when he came on board. Consequently, he has the sort of freedom that most people dream of. He reports to his boss regularly but not frequently. Why is this? The outcomes are there. When the results are there, provide freedom.

There are other people who also desire maximum freedom; in fact, that probably describes most people. However, they have not yet developed the ability to work without you. They need your structure, some level of accountability to you, and more detailed requirements. This is no criticism; it is how leaders deal with reality. My advice to leaders of these people is to give them a little more freedom than you are comfortable with and see what they do with it, unless it means some unacceptable risk, financially or otherwise. Let them know that it is a trial period. Either they will show, over time, that they are able to use the autonomy in productive ways, or their behavior will reveal that they need more structure from you. I think this is the best direction because then, instead of blaming poor results on a micromanaging boss, they see the results as residing in themselves. You want to increase their independence to the maximum as long as it is accompanied by their increased ownership.

6. Challenge

You need to challenge those you lead. By challenge, I refer to the amount of stretching, risk, and discomfort that is required to meet high goals and visions. As the marketplace realities dictate, businesses don't remain static—they grow or die. This is actually true in any organizational context: NGOs need to constantly look for new ways to meet needs. Churches need to spend time seeing how their message and vision can be better conveyed. Counselors need to be attending workshops to increase their skill sets. So challenge is an essential part of leadership. But you need to figure out what the right amount of challenge will be. Whether it's in promotions, bonuses, quotas, or team goals, you are to set challenges that work for you and your people.

Challenge is stressful by its very nature. It causes discomfort, but this is not necessarily a bad thing. Psychological and medical research shows that certain levels of stress are good for us: living with deadlines, having to prepare for a speech, needing to be on time to a meeting. Such challenges raise our adrenaline and cortisol hormone levels. They alert us and heighten our awareness. They require more of us than is normal, so we are able to stretch and perform at a higher level. This sort of stress, in the right dosages, increases our abilities, competence, and results. Challenge is how top athletes break world records.

However, too much challenge, causing too much stress, can be debilitating. If the stress level is too high or goes on for too long, people not only become discouraged, but they can even experience physical health problems. On a management level, you have probably seen that when someone has a goal that is just impossible, the result is not good for them. Challenge helps, but once you reach the level beyond discomfort into actual inability, things begin to break down.

On the other side of the equation, too little challenge and stress is not a formula for leadership success either. Without challenge, we tend to stay in the comfort zone. People punch in, go through the routine, and punch out. That is also just human nature. If you have a stable organization with mediocre goals, you might think a no-challenge mentality might work. But who wants to lead people to mediocrity? Not only that, the no-challenge mentality doesn't work in reality because of the grow-or-die principle. As they say, organizations and teams grow or die; there is no middle ground.

Your task is to motivate the right ratio of challenge: beyond comfort, and stopping before inability and discouragement. You can do part of that task by creating a context for passion, as I discussed earlier. People who feel a passion inside don't mind challenge. In fact, they are internally driven to meet challenges. They don't need you to motivate them. They need you to provide a structure for them to push themselves toward the goal.

Another relational aspect to effective challenge is understanding and training your people's stance, or attitude, toward challenge. As a leader, you need to create a culture that sees challenge as good for everyone, and you need to make sure that challenge is seen as normal reality. It isn't a new project to try, nor a way to make people work harder. It's the way organizations are.

You have to understand how those you lead see challenge. This is a highly relational ability. People have different stances toward the stress of challenge. Some people simply see life that way in the first place, and that is a good thing. These people tend to take high ownership of their lives. They associate both their success and their failures with themselves and don't blame the outside world. They see the value of goals that stretch them and use what they have learned even if they don't reach a goal. These individuals are your allies in challenge. Like those with passion, you really don't need to motivate these people as much as you need to create the system that helps them achieve. And when you have a person with high ownership as well as a positive stance toward challenge, clone her! She is gold.

I have a friend who is like this. He eats challenges for breakfast. He started working for an automotive parts company when he was a teenager. He stayed with the company a long time and took every challenge the owner could throw at him. He was doing inventory, sales, accounting—everything. The owner set all kinds of goals for him, seeing the type of young man my friend was. He was constantly being stretched and tested. If there were goals he failed to achieve the first time, he did his homework and then succeeded the second time. He was a dream. Of course, as the years passed, this caused a major problem for the owner. My friend was likely to set up his own shop across the street. But the owner was smart enough to solve his problem by offering my friend a partnership that continues to this day, very successfully.

Some, however, will come into your leadership sphere with less enthusiasm toward challenge. They will resist it, not being comfortable with "being uncomfortable." Some will resent it and think you are pushy and domineering. Some will take it personally, as if you should be giving them perks because you like them. And some will be overwhelmed and hesitant, often due to their own life stresses or personal difficulties.

Most of the time, these people can be trained to accept and see the value of challenge. It may require conversations in which you listen and understand their resistance. But at the same time, over and over again, you let them know that this is normal, expected, and good. It's the way it is, it won't change, and you believe in them.

There will always be a percentage of people who are, for whatever reason, stuck in the desire to stay in the comfort zone. They will see all stress as a bad thing. They are stalled in that position. Certainly you should do your due diligence of working with them on taking the challenges. Some will get on track. But, after that, it's probably fruitless to spend 80 percent of your time with the 20 percent who don't want to get it. It may be best to, as the saying goes, assist them in the process of making some other organization successful.

I once had dinner with a successful man who actually told me that one of his major goals in life was to have zero stress! I had a hard time figuring out how, having that stance, he achieved what he achieved because he had done a lot. Finally, as I got to know him, I understood that he had a say-do disconnect. He wasn't living what he said. In actuality, he was a very goal-driven, challenge-based person whose talent and motivation levels made him successful. Though he talked about having zero stress, in reality, this was more of a fanciful dream of one day having nothing to do but sit in a hammock and drink lemonade, than the reality of his day-to-day life. In general, you don't see success in people who don't live out challenge, though it always involves stress. So use your relational skills to build this ability into your people.

7. Performance Feedback

As you know, you need some sort of system or process to evaluate the progress of those you lead. Whether it be a monthly performance appraisal, an annual review, or another mechanism, this is a necessary part of formal leadership. Part of what you do involves measuring progress, evaluating goals, addressing problems, and coaching. While a great deal of performance feedback involves objective information, your relational skills can play a large role in making this a valuable and helpful process.

Performance feedback applies to any type of organizational structure, and it needs to fit that type. For example, a nonprofit organization might have a more informal way of letting its volunteers know how they are doing because there are no hard-data consequences, such as the presence or absence of a raise, a bonus, commission, or stock options. Volunteers are there because they believe in the mission of the organization, and they can leave anytime they feel like it. Remember that if you lead volunteers. Although they need feedback, your job is also to help them stay as motivated and engaged as possible.

So how do you give performance feedback in a relationally productive way? First, you need to *normalize the evaluative process itself.* That is, often performance feedback is not seen as a necessary, positive, or integrated part of the job. Instead, it is sometimes approached with fear and loathing, on the part of the evaluator as well as the one being evaluated. You have most likely seen things come up such as performance anxiety, fear of one's flaws being exposed, fear of criticism, anxiety about losing a friendly working relationship, shame, and even fear of losing a position. No one ever really enjoys negative performance feedback, but it can be a more positive experience if done well.

Next, *talk to the person ahead of time about the process.* If it's a formal performance review, make sure the person knows when the review is scheduled and what it's about. The tendency is that fear and anxiety increase over time before an event such as this. However, knowing that you recognize a review can be stressful and that as the evaluator you understand the anxiety can make the person's anticipation much easier to bear. The result can be that the review itself is less likely to be influenced by emotion and more likely to focus on the real issues. So prior to any scheduled performance review or feedback session, ask your direct report what she anticipates might happen in that conversation and then ask what she thinks about it. This doesn't have to be anything emotional at all. It's just considerate listening, which can help the feedback conversation go better.

When giving feedback, it is important to *acknowledge the underlying causes for any reached or unreached goals.* That is, hitting the numbers is great. Missing the numbers is something you want to pay attention to. But there are reasons he did or didn't hit them. If you help him see what he did or didn't do, he is much more likely to produce better results next time. It's never about the numbers *only.* Numbers exist as a signal to point to causes you can change and modify. There could be areas such as resourcing, skill set, fit, time management, discipline and structure, attitude, personal circumstances, and the like. Use your own relational abilities to dig a little, helping him to see you as a partner in his becoming successful.

I was working with an executive who was unpacking all the aspects of his work life, in order to analyze each one and see what could be improved. One of those aspects was his work relationship with his executive assistant. This is a key position for an executive, as the assistant is the glue that holds his work life together. Her tasks included organizing him, monitoring his projects, and representing him to the world. Though she was well-trained and highly competent, he still thought that they weren't maximizing the potential of their work together. It seemed to him that the two of them could achieve more effectiveness in their work relationship.

By this time, I had enough of an understanding of the executive, his role, and how he ticked, so I interviewed his assistant as well. She was pretty much top shelf. But as I got to understand her work relationship with him, I realized that there was an area of improvement based on their professional relationship. It had to do with his work context. The nature of his work required him to travel a good deal, both driving and flying to different locations. It demanded more "face time" with people in different locations, so he spent as much time on the road as he did at his office.

As often happens, the executive would call his assistant while he was driving, or at airports in between flights, in order to catch up and make real-time decisions. This was fine, except that she never knew how much time she had to go over the to-do list with him. She didn't know if he had one minute or thirty. Without that knowledge, she didn't know whether to give him the overview or the details. And her anxiety caused her to get flustered and make mistakes, which was frustrating for both of them. Not wanting to add to her boss's pressures, she didn't say anything to him about it and tried to handle the anxiety herself.

It was a relatively simple matter to tell both of them that he would improve effectiveness with her if, whenever he called, he would start by saying, "I have this much time." They were both relieved and liked the idea. We then, however, went a step further into the cause. I said to him, "That's fine, but the problem is that there are most likely several more things like this that she is afraid to talk to you about, and I want you to let her know it's okay." And I said to her, "I want you to speak up about these matters; it's for his benefit." To me, they had a relational problem at the core: the assistant was afraid to speak up, and the executive, simply by being a busy person, was oblivious to her discomfort.

The point of this story is to drive home the fact that effective performance feedback acknowledges underlying causes of the wins, and of the losses. If we had just ended with the boss saying, "I'll tell you how much time I have," the assistant would not have been able to deal with her fears of bringing up problems, and while one symptom would improve, a whole host of other issues would have gone unaddressed.

Finally, it is important that you *hear the person's responses to the appraisal*. The review process goes well when everyone is on the same page on performance and goals. But it is common for the person being led to have differences, feelings, or other perspectives on what is going on. If you refuse to hear and understand those concerns, you run the risk of negating any value in the process. When people feel misread, yet don't feel permission to clarify what they experience, they simply tune out the leader on the inside while nodding and taking notes on the outside.

Every perceptive leader has had this experience: she does the review, makes her points, and gives advice. The person she is working with seems to be tracking, but she knows something is wrong: the lights are on, but nobody's home. This is the time to use your relational skills to ask and probe: "I need to know what you think about what the review is saying." "I don't mind disagreement; in fact, it will help the process." In most cases, the other person's response will not make a significant difference in the appraisal or the steps to take. But it will make a huge difference in how cooperative the person is in following up. People who feel heard are more prone to go the extra mile.

Don't Set Yourself Up to Be Blindsided

Using your relational world is a significant part of leading with intuition. However, it doesn't mean becoming a counselor instead of a leader or a boss. It's about being what and who you were designed to be in the first place: a relationally based person. And it's about using your relational abilities to "read the landscape." This will help you to not be blindsided by the decisions and reactions of those you lead.

Leaders who shortcut or avoid the relational aspects of their role are surprised when people become distant, resentful, or just leave. Relational leaders see the signs coming a long way off and have time to take corrective measures. Even more importantly, however, they are the ones who—because they take the time to connect—instill confidence, hope, and trust in people, who then give their all to achieving the vision.

PART V

TRANSFORMATION

GROWING AS A LEADER

On June 15, 2006, Microsoft Corporation announced that its founder and chairman, Bill Gates, would transition out of a day-to-day role in the company into more involvement with the Bill and Melinda Gates Foundation, a philanthropic organization that focuses on global health and education. At the time, there was intense interest and speculation about why Gates would make this move during a time of history-making success in his business and leadership. Some people theorized that he was getting out at a strategic time because competition was finally catching up with the organization. Others said the move was because his colleagues at Microsoft had become better at running things than he had. Whatever the reasons may have been, it seems clear that Gates had a consistent and real desire to become involved in the bigger picture of life. He wanted to have an additional impact on his world, to lead in a different vein. In other words, *he was intentional about moving and directing his life and his leadership to the next level.*

Back when Gates made this decision, those who questioned it thought this move might be misguided and costly, and that Gates would squander his considerable influence. It turned out that the critics were wrong. Over time, his decision has undeniably magnified his ability to make a difference in the world. Consider just a few of the figures that document the work of the Bill and Melinda Gates Foundation around the world:

- 7.3 million people have received antiretroviral treatment for HIV/AIDS.
- The number of cases for ten serious tropical diseases dropped from 3.5 million in 1986 to 22 cases in 2015.
- 450 million mosquito nets have been distributed to combat malaria.
- 3 million households have received access to drought-tolerant maize.[1]

This is not at all to dismiss Gates's contributions to the world of technology and business. He has made a tremendous difference and improvement in how the world communicates and works. But when an experience touched him at a deeper level, it changed the direction of his life and the focus of his leadership. In an interview with Charlie Rose, Melinda Gates described how everything changed the day her husband visited a tuberculosis hospital in Africa:

We often call each other when we are on the road. Almost every day. But it was a different call. Bill was really quite choked up on the phone . . . because he'd seen firsthand in a TB clinic hospital how awful it is to have that disease. . . . He literally said to me, "It's a death sentence. To go into that hospital is a death sentence." So he decided not just to donate money to that one hospital, but to do things that could help thousands and millions get out of poverty altogether.[2]

The emotional impact of this experience was

transformative for Gates. The word *transform* encompasses something different and more profound than mere change. To be transformed is to experience a thorough reorientation, something that happens from the inside out. Think of it this way: We *change* a house with a paint job; we *transform* a house with a remodel. Transformation is a makeover in the deepest part of yourself, and it results in a whole new perspective on life, which in turn leads to new ways of behaving and revitalized values about life and leadership.

The Bible places a strong emphasis on transformation. In fact, it isn't considered optional—for a leader or for anyone who chooses to follow Christ. When speaking of transformation, New Testament writers often use the Greek word *metamorphoo.* It is the word used by Matthew to describe the transfiguration of Christ: "Jesus' appearance was transformed so that his face shone like the sun, and his clothes became as white as light" (Matthew 17:2 NLT). The apostle Paul charges his readers to "be transformed by the renewing of your mind," and describes our relationship with Christ as one in which we "are being transformed into his image" (Romans 12:2; 2 Corinthians 3:18). *Metamorphoo* is also the root of the English word *metamorphosis,* a process that involves much more than growth (becoming larger, stronger, or wiser, for example). Metamorphosis is a complete change from one state to a higher state: a caterpillar becomes a butterfly and a tadpole becomes a frog. Paul writes about the Christian journey in a similar way, "Therefore, if anyone is in Christ, the new creation has come: The old has gone, the new is here!" (2 Corinthians 5:17).

As a leader, you certainly do need to make external changes, and doing so adds great value in your organization. But you cannot ignore the need for internal change. Transformation is truly leadership from the gut, for it requires much more than honing your skills, following best practices, or implementing latest leadership strategies. It literally requires your entire being, energies, and life. And it requires a commitment to the process of transformation—a willingness to embrace a lifestyle of ongoing growth and change from the inside out.

Chapter 10

PERSONAL GROWTH IS

LEADERSHIP GROWTH

Andrew leads a staff of six in a small nonprofit that designs solar-powered water purification systems for use in communities without electricity. The days are always full and he enjoys helping his staff with problem solving. However, in recent months it's become routine for him to lose an hour or more a day to interruptions and last-minute meetings. To accommodate the needs of his staff and still get his own work done, Andrew decides to come in an hour earlier each day.

The good news is that Andrew identified a challenge and made a positive change to improve things. But it's a change that came with a cost: he has now lost an hour he could otherwise spend at home with his family or doing something he enjoys, such as working out. So, in making a change to address a work problem, he has actually created another problem in his personal life. In order to move beyond change toward transformation, Andrew needs to go deeper and consider *why* he has this challenge in the first place. Why does he lose so much productivity time to the tyranny of the urgent? An hour a day is not insignificant lost time.

Let's suppose that through a coaching relationship, Andrew realizes that although he loves his mission and his people, he has difficulty saying no to their last-minute requests, especially when they come at the end of the work day. Instead of saying, "I need to go, but let's handle this tomorrow," he stays as long as it takes to help them out. While his commitment to his staff is admirable, his coach suspects there might be more to it. When asked why he can't seem to say no, Andrew admits that he is afraid of disappointing his team.

As Andrew keeps digging into the why behind his fear, he realizes that throughout his career, and even before that in his family growing up, he has always struggled with setting time boundaries with people. He struggled with feeling like he was letting people down, or that he wasn't there for his staff when they needed him. That's when the lights come on for him. Instead of just making an external change (coming in an hour earlier), he needed to make an internal change—to face his fear and let go of his compulsive need to avoid disappointing his staff. It is not easy and it requires work, but with the help and support of his coach, he slowly experiences a transformation. Instead of leading from a place of fear (*I am afraid of letting people down*), Andrew began to lead from a place of health and strength (*I can and will take responsibility for how I spend my time and energy*).

Do you see the difference between change and transformation in this scenario? In making a change, Andrew focused on his circumstances; in pursuing transformation, he focused on himself. While change was limited to addressing external issues, transformation required addressing internal issues and pursuing personal growth. Then he could address his circumstances in a way that reinforced and supported his leadership and his values.

God created human beings with an innate desire for growth and change. That means that you are actually designed for the purpose of transformation. This spiritual spark within is what motivates your desires to improve, grow, and achieve in all aspects of life: leadership, love, work, self-development, and purpose. This part of you is not satisfied with the status quo. It draws you to be increasingly transformed into the person God made you to be, a process that happens as you are "transformed by the renewing of your mind" (Romans 12:2).

If you consistently pursue personal growth and transformation, you will continue to be on the path of change and improvement in your leadership. That's when transformation itself becomes a way of life, and it will inevitably change how you lead others. You will be rooted in the present, but also looking to the future, at how you can be not merely a *better* person or leader, but a fundamentally *different* one.

Transformation of your inner world is what ties together all of the other parts of leadership we've already explored: values, thoughts, emotions, and relationships. You are not designed to be static, carved in stone, or finished for good. You are created to grow: to mature in and hone your values, to increase the complexity of your thoughts, to develop your emotional repertoire, and to operate as a highly relational leader. Transformation, the process of developing the growing part of you, integrates all the aspects of your inner world. This is the essence of leading from your gut.

Transformational leadership certainly isn't a new idea. In fact, it has been a well-researched and valuable concept for some time.[1] However, the phrase tends to be used to distinguish between simply managing others or inspiring them to high performance. In this chapter, we'll focus instead on a more specific and focused aspect of transformation. It has to do with your personal development as a leader, not merely the way you lead.[2] When you are intentional about growing as a person, you will begin to lead from a different perspective and attitude.

Having worked with many leaders over the years, I have discovered three initiatives that are especially effective in helping leaders to prioritize their personal growth and transformation. The first is about intentionality, the second is about self-awareness, and the third has to do with dealing effectively with time.

1. Engage Intentionally in Growth

Personal growth and transformation happen in a variety of ways, but intentional growth requires structure. That is, your internal world needs relationships and tasks in which it can be connected, strengthened, understood, guided, and even healed. Intentional growth is well worth the time, and it can also prevent many small problems from becoming serious ones.

There are many ways to create a structure or plan for growth—from a coaching or mentoring relationship that gets "under the skin," to a small group, or professional counseling, depending on the situation and need. The point is, as a leader, you need a structured relationship in which you can work on yourself, not just your leadership skills. And that relational context translates into better leadership for you. Having a dedicated context and structure just for your internal work is the heart of growing and transforming.

Personal transformation is not something you can do alone. It requires relationship with other people, either individually or in a group. You simply don't possess the elements you need, within yourself, to grow in significant ways. You need acceptance and safety from others so you can face difficult realities. You need support and feedback in order to see what is going on inside you. You need perceptive people who can help you look at your blind spots. You need guidance and wisdom from others who understand the process of growth and transformation so you don't take more wrong turns than you need to. And you need others who understand and identify with what growing and leadership are all about since leadership and growth require others who "get it." So make sure that whatever you engage in on a growth level includes safe, accepting, honest, and competent people: the kinds of people you can trust and who are like the person you want to become as well.

Once you have a relational structure, the next task is to identify the personal growth areas you need to work on. Sometimes the issues you need to work on will be obvious, but not always. It's not uncommon for people to feel a bit unclear about where to start in their growth. To help get you started, the next section covers a few common growth areas that many leaders choose to focus on.

Common Growth Areas

A growth area is an aspect of your character that needs significant improvement. I define character as "that set of capacities required to meet the demands of reality." The leader has many demands on his or her plate: financial, performance, and organizational culture, to name a few. And the extent to which the leader possesses and utilizes the right capacities to meet those demands is largely the extent to which the leader succeeds. Simply put, a growth area is anything within you that needs to be transformed so that you can live, relate, lead, and perform to the best of your ability.

A large part of the growth process has to do with being able to tackle underlying issues that tend to get in the way of both leadership and life. That means identifying the areas in which we are not yet where we need to be, and taking the necessary steps to address those issues. Here are some examples of common growth issues leaders need to deal with and successfully resolve.

Self-sufficiency. Although it's often part of the warp and woof of a leader's training, the tendency to be an independent person is a liability, not an asset. You need to have a few significant relationships in your life, often unrelated to your leadership and your work, in which you can let your hair down and be vulnerable on a regular basis. Self-sufficiency is a valuable asset when it gives you freedom to make choices. But it becomes a liability when it hampers your ability to trust other people on a deep and vulnerable level.

Grow your ability to let others in and depend on them, not only for advice but simply for their presence. Leaders who learn to lean on a few people can in turn be leaned on by many. Leaders who can't lean on anyone are at risk of not reaching their potential. This is why we dealt with the importance of good relational images in chapter 8.

Over-responsibility. The tendency to take on too many burdens is an important personal growth issue for leaders. They lean toward taking responsibility for others' choices, failures, and even well-being. You can't be a life-support system for everyone. The growth process can help you learn how to clearly define yourself and your role, so that you are doing what only you can do and letting others take ownership of their lives.[3]

It is a transformational experience to understand where over-responsibility comes from, how strong it can be, what it has to do with significant relationships, and how great a part guilt plays. Over-responsible leaders can often, with a little work and support, learn to set the limits in the right places, deal with their fears, and move into higher levels of functioning and influence.

Inability to confront. Successful leaders confront well; that has long been established. However, when the seminars and workshops on effective confrontation don't produce the results you want, it is often because the problem is a personal growth issue—a transformational matter rather than a skills matter.

The process of growth can go a long way to resolve an inability to confront, so that you either learn how to confront or can make better use of confrontation training. Often, I find that leaders have long-standing fears of letting people down, injuring them, having them withdraw, or experiencing their anger. These fears must be dealt with to see improvement in this important ability.

So how do you identify your own growth issues? Perhaps the simplest way is to do what I call "tracing the root of the bad fruit." Jesus provided the foundation for this principle when he said, "A good tree cannot bear bad fruit, and a bad tree cannot bear good fruit" (Matthew 7:18). Start by naming some difficulty in your life and leadership, and then look to see what issue within you might be driving it. For example, bad fruit might be a revolving door of staff or volunteers leaving your organization. The root or character cause of that (barring events external to you, such as market or financial changes) could be any number of things, such as a tendency for you to gloss over negative issues, micromanage and control others, or not being confrontive in healthy ways.

You might say, "Oh, I know this part, it's about my strengths and weaknesses. I've had assessments and I know mine." Actually, character growth is not the same as working on strengths and weaknesses, and it will help here to consider the differences between the two.

Strengths and Weaknesses

There is a great deal of research on leadership strengths and weaknesses. A significant contribution of thought—represented by major voices such as Peter Drucker[4] and Marcus Buckingham and Donald Clifton[5]—says that it makes more sense to invest time and energy in developing your personal strengths and your people's strengths, rather than developing your weaknesses. That is, you are wasting time trying to make a numbers person into a marketing person and vice versa. The research seems to clearly demonstrate that the best direction is to build on what is strong and to manage what is weak.

There is an important contextual issue here, though. We need to make a distinction once more between externals and internals. Focusing on strengths works only when dealing with externals—leadership skills, competencies, talents, and gifts. When it comes to internals—our character, growth issues, and our ability to relate—we do not have the option to *manage* weaknesses; we need to resolve them.

A character weakness is not part of our hardwiring in the same way that our gifts and talents are. We weren't designed to be self-sufficient, over-responsible, or unable to confront. Those weaknesses come from our significant relational experiences, our backgrounds, and our own choices. So when we talk about character, we do not have to manage or accept as a fatalistic reality that we will always be this way because we have always been this way. There is always hope for growth and transformation. The growth process works. It works with personal character weaknesses and issues. I have seen it work with thousands of people over the years, many of them leaders.

For example, one business leader, Brad, asked me to help him strengthen his people management skills. Brad didn't take the initiative to come see me; his boss sent him to me. The boss was concerned that Brad, though a well-trained, hard worker with a good set of ethics, simply turned people off who worked under him. He couldn't light a fire under others. They didn't *not* like him, but they didn't really like him, either, and it was affecting the culture of the organization. When we sat down, Brad said, "I don't think I'm a people person. I'm wondering if I need to move to a more technical area."

This is a reflection of the mistaken hardwiring thinking: *I'm not good with people. I'm just that way.* For Brad, it was an unnecessary fatalistic stance about his character weaknesses.

As I continued to interview Brad, it became clear that he had a weakness in the area of self-sufficiency, mentioned above. He had grown up in a high-functioning, intact family of positive people. At the same time, however, his family culture had no place for need and dependency. He couldn't lean on anyone when he was lonely or afraid. Instead, the message was be strong, and go for it. It was the right message when Brad needed courage but the wrong message when he needed comfort and support. The more we looked at this, we saw that Brad looked at work and leadership as something that was supposed to be entirely self-motivating, and he had to come up with his own answers. For Brad, it was all about willpower and trying harder, not drawing on others for help.

It didn't take long for Brad to see this weakness and take the transformational steps he needed to overcome it. He found an executive support group in which the members discussed both work issues and personal issues, and it was very helpful for him. Brad experienced the integrative reality that he could be competent, connected, and inspiring. He moved out of his self-sufficient state and began to be connected relationally. As you might imagine, this transformation then translated to his leadership. He was better able to read his people and understand them, while at the same time inspiring and holding them to high standards.

The point here is that if you have a character flaw or issue, there is no reason you should simply surrender to it. You can make great improvements on a transformational level. Character weaknesses—as opposed to competency weaknesses or styles—are meant to be transformed, not tolerated.

2. Become Self-Observant

To access the growing part of you, you also need the ability to self-observe. It is important that you acquire the habit of regularly looking at what you do, and how you do it. Psychologists call this capacity the *observing ego,* and it is a very helpful part of your mind. In self-observation, you dispassionately monitor your behaviors, words, emotions, and attitudes. And you do this *without criticizing or judging.* The task in the moment is simply to observe, to watch yourself from a distance, as if you were a character in a movie. You can observe positive as well as negative aspects of yourself. You can notice that you are a better listener than you thought, and that feels encouraging. Or you can notice that you give people way too much time to ramble and talk when you have time-critical tasks to engage in. Or you can notice both of these in the same conversation—I certainly have! Then, having observed what you are doing, you are more able to address whatever needs to be transformed.

Self-observation is often a catalyst for personal growth. We engage in changing what we observe, what we know, and what we experience. Let's take a look at three keys to effective self-observation.

Observe How You Affect Others

We are all like stones thrown into a river. Our attitudes and actions have a ripple effect that impacts all those around us. This is especially true with leaders. We make a difference in the attitudes, thoughts, and values of those we lead. You must pay close attention to the effect you have on others, or you will cease to have the impact you desire. That is why the chapters in part 4 on your relational world are so critical for you as a leader. The more relational you are, the better you can see your impact on others.

For example, a corporate executive I know was so committed to self-observation that he became highly attuned to the nuances of his direct reports. He once told me, "I knew I had come down too hard on Sam at the meeting. I reviewed the meeting in my mind afterward and saw myself grinding unnecessarily on him. And Sam became a little reserved, enough that I noticed he was acting differently toward me. So we talked afterward, and I was right. I hadn't motivated him; I discouraged him. I apologized, and we're okay now. But I would have missed that before I paid attention to how I impact others."

This may sound like a little thing. The direct report was a mature and experienced professional also. He would have dealt with the discouragement and moved on. He didn't need handholding. But look at the other side: by spending a couple of minutes being self-observant, the executive was able to invest a little time in a valuable person and resolve a little thing that could have become a big thing later.

Observe Your Strengths

Transformation for the leader is primarily about attending to behaviors or attitudes that aren't working well, but you can do a lot of good for yourself by also noticing when you are crushing the ball. Improving even more on what we excel at in our character can be highly productive. Someone who can help her team admit flaws without shame or guilt can learn, with the proper information and coaching, to do this even better. That's one reason I love these words written by the apostle Paul, "And we all, who with unveiled faces contemplate the Lord's glory, are being transformed into his image with ever-increasing glory, which comes from the Lord, who is the Spirit" (2 Corinthians 3:18). Moving from one state of "glory" to a higher state of "glory" is a good thing.

Observe Your Weaknesses

We wouldn't need to be self-observant if we always batted a thousand. The observing ego can certainly help us celebrate our improvements, strengths, and successes, but the larger benefit is in observing and addressing our mistakes. This is sometimes difficult for leaders who are under tremendous pressure to produce results. And many leaders tend to be highly self-critical, so the idea of looking at mistakes can be very uncomfortable. Then there are some leaders who live exclusively for the good news about themselves; they aren't aware of the negative, which is a form of narcissism.

Whatever the reason, you must be able to face and deal with your weaknesses. *The negative realities about yourself that you avoid today are the same ones that can ruin your leadership tomorrow.* You are better off the sooner you become accustomed to this reality. It will be worth it. Remember Randy, the CEO in chapter 2 who could deal with his misdemeanors but not his felonies? Have enough grace and courage to look at your felonies—your major flaws and errors—as well as your minor ones. You will then be in a position to experience transformation.

Observe Yourself in the Present

Your ability to observe what you are doing *as you are doing it* is invaluable. The shorter the time lapse between what you do and when you notice it, the better your adjustments and self-corrections. This is also called being "in the moment." The task is not as easy as it may sound. Leaders can be so future-minded that they miss what is going on around them. I knew, for example, that a small business owner friend of mine was on a transforming path when he said to me while I was talking to him, "Sorry, I wasn't listening just now. I was thinking about a cash flow issue I'm working with." It was a good sign that he was observing *at that time* what he was doing.

Be a self-observer. Don't let a day go by in which you haven't spent a few minutes replaying the videos of your actions and conversations with people. Notice the patterns and deal with them.

3. Make Time Your Ally

Growth takes time. Becoming a new and improved person is not instantaneous. It is a day-by-day process you need to adjust to and commit to for the long haul in order to achieve the transformational results you want to see. For leaders, the growth process generally takes more time than you planned for. But as with anything else in life, you get what you pay for. If growth were quick and easy, you would have already accomplished all you needed by now. And if you have been in leadership for any significant amount of time, you are aware that building anything meaningful, whether an infrastructure, a business model, or a team, requires a diligent and time-consuming process.

We all have friends who shine like a comet for a few months, perhaps even years, and then they crash and quickly move on to the next big thing. They live in an instant world and expect instant results. When those don't happen, they move on. You invest energy and resources in these people to your peril. But a wise leader invests instead in those who take their work and growth seriously and steadily improve over time.

The same wise principle—let's call it "seriously and steadily"—applies with your own growth and transformation. You want to be a good investment for your own efforts: steady, not a flash in the pan.

However, at the same time, we are responsible to take control of the time we have. Growth still has its own pace, and it is bigger than you and me. The biblical principle is that there is a season for everything in life: "A time to plant and a time to uproot" (Ecclesiastes 3:2). We simply have to do our part and trust that growth will happen. And as every gardener knows, we can't rush these seasons. God is in charge of the growth process, whether it be in our organization, our family, or our personal life.

This is often the most difficult aspect of growth for the leader. You don't have a lot of time; it is a resource that is quite limited. You can't increase the amount of time in your life. And you have multiple demands competing for the limited time you do have. But there is no microwave system for personal growth.

Imagine you broke a bone in your body. If you refused to rest and to do the necessary physical therapy, you could slow the regrowth and healing of the bone. But even if you did the rehab perfectly, it would still take weeks or even months before the bone would be mended and your body back to 100 percent. You would need to be patient, not think a lot about it, and be involved in the other meaningful aspects of life and work while the healing process took its own course. The same principle applies to your internal growth and healing. As you do the right things, in time, you will see the transformation—and the results.

The Value of Time

Why is time such a necessary part of the transformation process? Because growth requires an ordered sequence of events in order to produce the results. You need this ordered sequence to be able to let others know who you are, on a values level, a leadership level, and a personal level. You need time in order to understand and dialogue with others about the information you receive. You need time in order to think about and digest what you are learning. And you need time in order to try out new ways of relating and leading, testing them out, making mistakes, learning from them, and always moving on toward excellence. Time gives you room and space to do the best job of making the most of the ingredients and practices of personal growth.

I was having dinner recently with a friend who operates in the corporate world. He told me about his own process of transformation, which involved trust and took time.

"I have always enjoyed working with people and resourcing them to help an organization grow," he said, "but several years ago, I got some feedback that surprised me. On condition of anonymity, people said they were afraid of me. They thought I was too rigid and critical and wouldn't tolerate any mistakes. At first I fought that impression, but I began to notice there was a lot of truth to it. So I got a good coach and started digging into it. What I found was that I tend to be extremely hard on myself, to the point of harshness, and it flows downhill to those who report to me.

"I decided that wasn't a good thing, so I thought that if I was just more aware of it, I could curtail it and be a more reasonable boss. That helped a little, but I still had the basic tendency. That was frustrating because I didn't want to spend the rest of my career trying to keep this critical and harsh part of me muzzled. That sounded like a lot of effort. *I wanted to not be that way.* So I started working on my own critical voice inside. I learned where it came from. How it developed. And I learned a lot about forgiveness, both giving it and receiving it. I learned to accept things the way they are. And I even had some emotions about all of this.

"It didn't happen overnight. It took time to talk to people, to think through matters, and to learn to give up certain things. I had to concentrate on this personal transformation for a while. But there's no question in my mind that it was worth it. The feedback I get now is much different than it used to be."

Put in the time. It will pay you back.

Your Tasks with Time

While you can't make the process of growth an instant one, you don't have to just sit there passively letting the clock tick in your transformation. There are some critical roles you can play that will help the growth process accomplish what it should.

Be active in the time. Use your time wisely and well. Don't waste it, and don't expect the process of time alone to solve things. Set a structure for growth and keep to it. The old saying "Time heals all things" is neither helpful nor true. Time, in and of itself, never transformed anyone, any more than looking at a business plan and expecting a successful business to become a reality in a year with no effort. So make sure the people, the expertise, the commitment to growth, and the resources are in place, and stay current with it. Make it a high priority. If you find that urgent matters continually get in the way, retool and start over, but don't get derailed.

Use different types of time. There is more than one way to use growth time. The most common model is a regularly scheduled meeting: weekly, biweekly, and so on. It's often quite helpful to add more intensive growth times periodically, such as a weekend retreat or an all-day session with a coach. These sorts of experiences can accelerate the growth process because of the concentrated nature of the work. The point is not to get stuck in a rut. Nothing is worse than a transformational path that becomes boring. That is simply an oxymoron. Changeups can help keep the process of growth compelling and productive.

Use time to measure growth and change. Though personal growth can't readily be measured on a daily basis, it can be measured on some basis. Sometimes benefits resulting from personal growth can be measured weekly, monthly, quarterly, or annually, depending on the task and issue. The work you put into becoming a different person should, at some point, bear observable fruit in your life and in your leadership. You may, for example, notice that you are more relational, more honest, clearer, more direct, and more compassionate. At the same time, there should be corollary improvements in your people and productivity.

When Time Is Your Enemy

By the same token, you may notice that significant amounts of time are passing with little or no fruit. That is important to understand also. There can be several reasons for this.

You are not experiencing enough grace, acceptance, and empathy. It is common for leaders to find support systems that are high on accountability and low on grace. So they show up, admit failure, and promise to do better; then they show up the next time, admit failure, and promise to do better, and so on. You need people giving you what I described in the previous chapter: grace, acceptance, and empathy. That is the fuel we all need to grow and do better.

The situation requires more sustained and more frequent effort. There are times in which the issue takes more effort and resources than you budgeted for. This may be because it is a long-standing attitude or habit or because it is a knottier problem than you first thought. You may need to increase the meetings and resources. Sometimes that is the simple problem—the situation requires more help.

You are working on the wrong solution. Sometimes we get on the wrong track and go down the road a bit before we realize that the lack of results means it's time to seek another solution. For example, a manager I worked with wanted to be less resistant to his boss's program. He saw himself as not being a team player and wanted a better attitude. We dealt with that perspective for a while, and things didn't get better. Finally, after getting more information from others who worked for the boss, the reality emerged that the boss was a controlling and hypercritical man. Anyone who tried to please him was doomed to failure. That being understood, a new solution came out: learning to manage, deal with, and appropriately confront a difficult boss. Because the job had many other benefits the manager valued, he chose to stay on, but with better control over his exposure to his boss.

You tend to demand instant results. Leaders must charge ahead for results in their work. It's just part of wearing the leadership hat: you want to be your best and highest self yesterday. But at the same time, you need to accept the realities of time. I think the best thing you can do about this is to get involved in the job you love, the mission you believe in, the people you connect with, and the personal growth process. The more immersed we are in real life, the faster time seems to pass.

Make time your friend, not your enemy. Time well spent can make the difference between success and failure.

Just in Case You Become Discouraged . . .

Leaders are "get it done" individuals. They like an objective, a plan, and specific action steps. And now you've read this chapter about changing from the inside out, and maybe you're wishing it outlined a checklist of clear steps rather than principles and guidelines you can use to identify your own next steps. That's a common challenge for many leaders who want to be all they can be, and to stop being what they no longer want to be. But the good news is that while the principles are not transformation themselves, *identifying and following your right next steps will lead you to the transformation.* So that's where you start. My friend who had to do some internal digging to fix his harshness still took some steps, right? The steps of getting around the right coach, of asking himself where the harshness came from, of putting together some important themes of his past, of entering into forgiveness. These are the steps that "put the patient on the operating table" of growth, so to speak. And then the surgery works.

A client of mine told me he was getting negative feedback on how he motivated his team. They liked him, but felt he didn't "get" them and so that decreased their engagement. When I attended his company's team meetings, I noticed that when someone shared a struggle, he had a tendency to avoid staying with the struggle, and instead tried to make them feel more positive. For example, "Dave, I know your best customer was poached by a competitor. But you know what, man? You're a great guy, you'll make it." Now, there are times when statements like this can help. We all need encouragement. But we also need to "mourn with those who mourn" (Romans 12:15). That's how they know we are "with" them, and they can better hear and take actions on our encouragements. His tendency to "put a Christmas bow on it" when someone shared a struggle alienated people.

I made him aware of the pattern. He thought at first that I didn't want him to be positive. But he finally started realizing that he had lots of anxiety about sadness and negative aspects of life, and he could not tolerate them well. He was simply more comfortable with the positive half of reality, and not the negative half. The problem is that leaders need to be conversant in both.

He meditated on Bible passages, such as the Romans 12:15, and also the apostle Paul's counsel about relating to "the God of all comfort, who comforts us in all our troubles, so that we can comfort those in any trouble with the comfort we ourselves receive from God" (2 Corinthians 1:3–4). He learned that his own negatives were okay, and no safe person would ever judge him. And in time, he was much more adept at "being with" the struggles of his team, who then increased their engagement—with him and with the organization's mission.

This is just another example of how transformation is doable. It works. Just take the next step.

Chapter 11

SPIRITUAL GROWTH IS

LEADERSHIP GROWTH

John is a good friend whom I have known for many years. In fact, we were roommates when he was in college and I was in grad school. He has a great story that involves himself, God, and leadership, and it provides insights and principles that are helpful for every leader who wants to grow spiritually.

John is a fourth-generation owner of a Texas cattle ranch. His family is in the oil and gas industry, but his father ran that part of the business himself and did nothing to prepare John for that sector of work. John discovered that he possessed strong abilities and passions for counseling. As a result, he completed graduate school, trained as a therapist, and became a respected and well-liked counselor in private practice while also managing cattle operations on the ranch. After a sustained drought forced the sale of their livestock operations, John became a full-time counselor at his church. A dedicated family man, he also spent a great deal of his time with his wife and kids. Life was good!

So John was very surprised one day when his father asked him for some help overseeing the family business and estate. Even though his father hadn't explicitly asked him to leave his counseling practice, John knew this would likely mean leaving behind an extremely satisfying career.

Now, put yourself in John's shoes for a moment. Many years ago, you walked away from a large enterprise that had been a central force for your family for three generations. You have found a great deal of satisfaction and fulfillment in a totally unrelated career. You are experiencing no if-only or what-if feelings about deciding to walk away from the family business; your career cup is full. No one in the world would have faulted

John for simply declining his dad's offer and continuing to live the productive and meaningful life he had crafted for himself. But that's not what he did—and that's what makes his story not only compelling, but also instructive for every leader who wants to grow spiritually and to lead from that growth.

In this chapter, we'll explore the connection between spiritual growth and leadership growth. It's a connection richly illustrated in the events and decisions John made following his dad's request, so we'll come back to his story a few times. My hope is that John's story and the principles this chapter presents will help you to find direction and encouragement for your own spiritual path as a leader.

Who We Are as Spiritual Beings

The word *spiritual* refers to the truth that there is another and greater reality than what you experience in your own skin. It speaks to something and someone beyond you and bigger than you. There is an aspect of life that transcends normal life. It can't be seen or quantified, but it is real.

In the Bible, the word *spiritual* comes from the Greek term *pneumatikos*. It conveys the reality that our own spirits are to connect with and follow God's Spirit. The apostle Paul uses *pneumatikos* when he writes, "Those who are *spiritual* can evaluate all things, but they themselves cannot be evaluated by others" (1 Corinthians 2:15 NLT, emphasis added). His statement points to the fact that the mature Christian is to be led and taught by the Spirit.[1] In this sense, the Christian leader—and any Christian—is to constantly seek out God's guidance and strength in all things.

Here's the bottom line: *all growth is spiritual growth.* Anything God is involved with is spiritual by definition. Henry Cloud and I address this in our book *How People Grow*:

> The Bible anchors God as the source of all growth. All the way through the Bible we read that everything we need in life comes from him, not from ourselves (Acts 17:28; 1 Cor. 4:7). This essential and defining reality

helps to humble us and make us dependent on God. . . . When we see that the Bible points to God for all growth, we understand that all growth is spiritual growth. From groups that study the Bible to those dealing with relationships to those helping people with depressions or addictions, everything that fosters growth is ultimately from God.[2]

This is why I believe so strongly that the leader's personal growth is deeply spiritual in nature. Sometimes when I am training Christian leaders, I will refer to personal growth as "horizontal spiritual growth," meaning it is largely about our relationships with other people. Then I refer to the leader's relationship with God as "vertical spiritual growth," which means it includes everything that helps us connect with God— from Bible reading and prayer, to following the Holy Spirit in faith and with obedience.

Both personal growth and spiritual growth are essential for transformation. The objective of growth—and the practices required to achieve it—is to help you become someone new. When transformation begins to happen, you are well on your way to becoming a different person and a different leader.

Four Spiritual Growth Principles for Leaders

Now that we've covered the big picture about the essential connection between spiritual growth and leadership growth, we're going to focus on four critical aspects of growing spiritually as a leader and how you can leverage them for your own growth and transformation.

Make Following God Your Primary Calling

As a leader, your spiritual life provides the answer to the question, "What am I here for?" God has a calling, a purpose, for each of us, which means we aren't lost in a random and chaotic universe: "'For I know the plans I have for you,' declares the LORD, 'plans to prosper you and not to harm you, plans to give you hope and a future'" (Jeremiah 29:11). God's calling for your life includes your leadership. If you are called to lead, then you have a mission. If you have a mission, God's plan is for you to make some sort of a positive difference in this world.

When it became clear that he would be taking over the family business, John went into a season of deep prayer and reflection. *Why should I give up a good and meaningful life for something I haven't been groomed to lead?* He thought long and hard about this.

The more John thought, prayed, and sought the counsel of wise friends, the clearer his answer to that question became: *If not me, who else?* John became captivated by the enormous potential of the family ranch to do good in the world, providing energy, minerals, jobs, and opportunities. He began to have a vision for all that could happen if he took on the responsibility of leading the family business.

That process of seeking and discernment resulted in John ultimately becoming convinced he had been called. Just as he had been called for a season to do therapy, he was now being called to take on the reins of the family business. As it was thousands of years ago when the prophet Isaiah answered God's call by saying, "Here am I. Send me!" (Isaiah 6:8), John said yes to his calling.

It's important to understand that John's decision did not come from a place of passion or interest, though that came later. It was simply following what he felt God was calling him to do. On the face of it, this might seem counterintuitive or perhaps even unwise because passion is essential for effective leadership (as we discussed in chapter 7). However, sometimes calling *precedes* passion. We see this in the Bible with leaders such as Moses and Gideon who initially showed no passion for the work that ultimately became their divine calling. Moses had spent forty years as a desert shepherd (and had a murder on his rap sheet) when God called him to lead the Israelites out of slavery in Egypt. Gideon, a middle-aged man who described his clan as "the weakest in the whole tribe of Manasseh" and himself as "the least in my entire family" (Judges 6:15 NLT), was hiding in a winepress threshing wheat when God called him to be a great warrior and commissioned him to rescue Israel from the cruel oppression of the Midianites. Although they had questions and wrestled with God for answers, both men were obedient to their callings and God used them to change their world.

Passion is a key trait of every great leader, but ultimately passion must bend the knee to obeying God's call. If you're not on the path God has for you and headed in the direction God has called you to go to, all the passion in the world will not make it the right path.

What does transformation look like in making following God your number one calling? Simply put, it is moving from the lower state of focusing on any motivation other than following God, to the higher state of focusing on obedience as your first and most important motivation. Other motivations—including passion, competency, and meaningfulness—are great, but they must ultimately bend the knee to "followship."

We may find out that we have interest in leading in some direction. I look at that as a way to get moving, because I believe God intends to use people who are doing something, not looking at their navel waiting for him to tell them their mission. But once we are moving, we need to make sure God has greenlighted our course because he desires it for us.

Whether you are new to leadership or a veteran, it is essential to be clear about your calling. Ask God to let you know if your current role is where he wants you to remain, or if he has other things in mind. I have seen many examples of God telling leaders, "Stay," and many more of God saying, "Go." Seek God's counsel and ask him to make you sure of your calling.

Ask for What You Do Not Possess

After John quit his counseling position and took up his new role, he worked hard to familiarize himself with the unique demands of the energy business as well as the needs of the organization. He initially turned to his father for guidance, but because his father was becoming more disengaged as he aged, he had little time or energy for grooming John. Then, a few years into his new role, John's father passed away. From there, John was left to figure things out on his own.

It was an overwhelming time for John. He felt unequipped for such a monumental task. He was highly engaged in learning how to run everything, from finances and deals to systems. He also knew he needed to grow the business—because of the "grow or die" principle—but he had no experience in how to develop the business model, the corporate vision, the leadership, or the culture. He possessed a quick mind and was highly responsible, but that was not enough. So he reached out in all the ways the Bible tells us to reach out for strength. He prayed and asked God for help. He found safe people who listened, understood, and encouraged him. He identified the areas in which he needed help, and found experts and coaches to train him. He assembled a talented executive team to walk with him. In the process, John became strengthened by God's "righteous right hand." He began to grow in competence and confidence that the organization was now moving in the right direction.

You likely don't need me to tell you that leadership demands everything you've got—your time, energy, blood, sweat, and tears. There are times when leadership can be very meaningful and fulfilling, but it can also be lonely and draining. You need a source of strength to help you make the sacrifices required to keep moving forward in pursuit of your mission. If you want to lead for the long haul, not a day should go by that you don't acknowledge your needs and weaknesses and ask for God's provision and strength. That's what God's leaders throughout the centuries have done—humbly turned to God as their ultimate leader and asked for his strength to walk the extra painful mile or to face a dangerous situation with courage. They have prayed, searched, submitted, and asked—and God has been there: "I will strengthen you and help you; I will uphold you with my righteous right hand" (Isaiah 41:10).

The principle of asking for what you do not possess is transformative because the support, wisdom, and strengthening we take in from the *outside* (from God and the right people) is what enables us to become different from the *inside*. The opposite of this transformative process is to go it alone, to attempt to be self-sufficient, and to feel weird about asking for help. Don't let a fear of being perceived as a weak person, or even pride, keep you from asking for what you need. In fact, weakness is actually a strength in God's program, as he told Paul, "My grace is sufficient for you, for my power is made perfect in weakness" (2 Corinthians 12:9).

Reflect for a moment on your current leadership situation. All of the successful Christian leaders I have met and worked with are keenly aware of areas in which they need strengthening, for example in finances, marketing, sales, operations, strategy, team building, or people skills. And they spend dedicated time with God being strengthened by God, and by those who have the training or the emotional intelligence to help them. I'm sure you are no different. It's not a fault to admit you have a weakness and need strengthening. But it is a fault to feel that you must always have it all together. Admit the need and the lack, and ask God for guidance. Then take action to get the courage, patience, focus, resources, and skills you need.

Learn to Trust in Anxious Times

Leadership is stressful. You are either dealing with the stresses of not losing, or the stresses of taking risks to be a winner. It is simply a norm of leadership. And stress creates anxiety.

Anxiety is fundamentally about control. It emerges when we feel out of control in some area: a bad financial report or team members quarrelling. The problem is that most leaders are control freaks at some level. We micromanage and resist delegating. We want to keep a very tight grip on ourselves and our organizations, which then adds to the anxiety. Anxious times can be debilitating to the performance and overall health of the leader.

Most leaders desperately need transformation in this area. While the "overcontrol" response to anxiety is a natural one, it is not a good one, and doesn't work over the long haul.

Over and over again in the Bible, God provides us with his antidote for anxiety. It is to hand over to him our concerns, especially those over which we have no control:

- "But seek first his kingdom and his righteousness, and all these things will be given to you as well. Therefore do not worry about tomorrow" (Matthew 6:33–34).
- "Do not be anxious about anything, but in every situation, by prayer and petition, with thanksgiving, present your requests to God" (Philippians 4:6).
- "Cast all your anxiety on him because he cares for you" (1 Peter 5:7).

Making an intentional choice to trust lowers anxiety and allows us to focus on that over which we actually do have control. Here is why trust is transformational: It is not "natural" in nature, and requires you do what is "spiritual" in nature. What we do that feels natural and normal is simply no guarantee that it is spiritual. But when a leader goes against the natural and simply chooses to surrender control to God, anxiety lessens.

John was no stranger to high anxiety during the early part of taking over the business. We had many conversations about this aspect of leadership. He took his responsibility and calling quite seriously, and the burden was constantly with him for many months as he was gathering his resources.

John's own transformation was that, over time, he moved steadily from a natural tendency to overcontrol under stress, toward the spiritual practice of letting go and letting God. When he was faced with overwhelming challenges, he searched for God's path and ways. When his anxiety let him doubt he was the right person for the mission, he went to his safe people to ask for input and guidance. Their reassurance that he was the right person in the right place, along with the reassurance of God, stabilized and steadied him. John's anxiety lowered and his confidence was strengthened over this period.

I have never met or worked with a truly successful leader who hasn't experienced some significant seasons of anxiety. The ones who are totally anxiety-free have, in my experience, not performed well over the long haul. I think this is because their lack of fear causes them to be overconfident in their decisions, and to miss the due diligence of risk assessment. A bit of anxiety can be a good thing.

So I am assuming that you, like the rest of us, experience times of anxiety when things are stressful. It is simply a normative part of the leader's life. If that is so, I suggest you try this simple habit I have developed and practice regularly.

Take a sheet of paper and write out 1 Peter 5:7: "Cast all your anxiety on him because he cares for you." Beneath the verse, write down the top five challenges in your life and leadership that are currently a source of anxiety. These might be concerns related to family, health, finances, work performance, relational concerns, etc. Then ball up the paper and throw it in the trash, saying, "I cast these cares on you, Lord, because you care for me." It is a physical way of expressing trust and of transferring burdens to the broad shoulders of God. I just did this while I was writing it, and I feel like I have lost ten pounds—a truly physical release of anxiety from the burdens I'm carrying. I hope this practice will help you to pursue transformation in connection with your own anxiety as well.

Cascade Your Transformation

Ultimately, how leaders grow spiritually should cascade into how they direct their people. In leadership, the word *cascade* refers to the process of passing downstream to others some vital vision, strategy, or habit. If we are aware of our growth areas and pursuing transformation, it goes without saying that we will be more prepared to lead well, but it doesn't stop there. Transformation is a gift that keeps on giving, and we need to be intentional about passing it along to those we lead. And in great leaders, that cascade of transformation goes beyond those they personally direct, to those who are directed by them, and on and on. Well-run organizations develop a culture of excellence and performance that runs down many levels, but it all begins at the top. What we sow, we reap.

When Jesus told Peter, "Feed my sheep" (John 21:17 NLT), he was speaking to him from a context of many, many lessons and experiences he had previously cascaded to Peter to prepare him for leadership. Although Peter made lots of famous mistakes, he learned enough from them to faithfully carry out the work Jesus entrusted to him, and to take his place as one of the founding fathers of the Christian faith. The lessons Peter learned, which we know through the stories written about him in the Bible and the books of the Bible he wrote, have continued to cascade down to believers for more than 2,000 years.

Leaders who fail to cascade their transformation tend to be highly competent in their own world but unwilling to pass on what is important to them. Because they keep their ideas, vision, and growth to themselves, they stop the flow of wisdom that otherwise could benefit those who report to them.

This problem is often rooted in a lack of confidence that one can deeply influence others, a fear that no one will really be moved to change. Transformation comes when leaders face this lack of confidence and fear and dedicate themselves to reaching out to the team and beyond. When leaders take the risk to convey what they believe and feel, people almost always connect and respond positively. Cascading has just occurred.

I say that this is transformation because I have so often seen how insecure leaders begin to feel confident and secure the more they face these fears. It is truly a change from the inside out. Such is the transformation I observed in John as he dealt with his challenges. As one who had spent most of his career as a counselor, he didn't have a great deal of cascading opportunities in his job. He practiced his craft well, but there was no team or larger organization to get on board.

He quickly realized that for the company to grow, he needed to reach out and convey what was important to him—to his team and to the company as a whole. His transformation was evident in how he collaborated with his core players to update the organization's mission and vision, core values, culture, and strategic plan. He then empowered them to implement these values and strategies and to pass them along to others. Although it was a process he had never previously experienced, it's one he now deeply enjoys. And his impact on others has become exponentially more powerful, which is the essence of cascading well.

Here is an action step you can take to get started on this aspect of the spiritual nature of leadership. Write down the top three lessons God has been teaching you in this season of life and leadership. The lessons may be connected to specific growth areas you've identified (as discussed in chapter 10), or to other issues you're learning more about, such as patience, diligence, courage, or how to listen better. Anything you're learning or hearing from God that has been impacting you is a good candidate for the list.

For each item on your list, come up with ways that you can cascade those valuable lessons to your team. God's lessons are universal to the human race, and passing them along to your people is a gift to them. You may want to talk about these lessons at the beginning of your team meetings, or have a separate meeting about them. You may want to have an offsite dedicated to growth. And you certainly want to be modeling these lessons in ways that are observable to your people. Walking the talk is always the most powerful cascade.

Most Christian leaders I work with in the for-profit world don't run explicitly Christian companies. That is, while they try to execute biblical principles of trust, responsibility, and excellence, they don't have Bible verses in their literature, prayer at meetings, and so forth. They prefer to run under the radar a bit, live out the gospel in their behavior, and have spiritual conversations on a more organic level when the time is right. Others, including leaders who work in churches and Christian nonprofits, are more explicit about their faith. One is not better than another, it's just a preference based on one's approach.

If you lead within a Christian context, you may want to cascade your lessons using biblical principles, your own testimony, and prayer. If not, your cascade may be more subtle about the lessons you are learning. I call it "leaving out the address" of the principles you're learning until there is time for a private conversation. Either way, you will lead well when you lead from how you have grown spiritually.

An Invitation to Integration

So what is happening with John and the company? He has consistently continued to follow God. His leadership team is becoming more cohesive, and there is great excitement about the future. Though there is often high stress, his anxiety is lower, especially as he finds himself tackling higher-level problems over time. And his organization is becoming an extension of the vision and values he has worked out with his people. John is reforming the family business into the kind of organization he believes God has called him to lead, and with his family, he is planning for the next few decades of growth and development. The engine is running, and good things are happening.

I mentioned earlier that John did not initiate his career change out of passion or interest, as he was happy and fulfilled where he was. It was a matter of obedience to a spiritual call. But here is the ironic thing. *The passion is now present.* John has become aware over the past few months and years that he has strong positive feelings that focus on the organization's new day. He has discovered strengths and capacities within himself that have helped him lead. While the work is hard and complex, he looks forward to engaging his tasks every day (well, almost every day).

Here is my point, and it is for all leaders: I believe that *God integrates all of who you are to accomplish all of what he calls you to do.* God designed you to fulfill some destiny, some purpose. He wants you to do it with all your capacities and all of yourself, to use your leadership to "Love the LORD your God with all your heart and with all your soul and with all your strength and with all your mind" (Luke 10:27).

He will not give you a call and then design your life so that it's drudgery and something you dread day after day. That may be how it feels at the beginning, as it did with Moses and Gideon. But over time, his purpose is better served by making sure you are 120 percent all in for the call, with your values, thoughts, emotions, relationships, and transformation. And that is ultimately the spiritual nature of what leadership is all about.

CONCLUSION

As someone who is involved in influencing others toward excellence and inspiration, you need to be the best you can be—for yourself, your mission, and for those you lead. Terry Ledbetter, a client who founded a successful insurance company, was committed to this for himself and asked me to work with him on both his leadership and his personal growth.

Most executives I work with already have high levels of competency in at least some of the five areas of this book—values, thoughts, emotions, relationships, and transformation. Terry was very strong in values and thoughts. He was driven by clear core value principles, and he was a brilliant business designer and strategist. But he quickly realized that he was not as developed as he needed to be when it came to emotions, relationships, and transformation. As I explained this model, he told me he wanted to grow and learn in each of these areas.

The results have been very positive. Terry now gets feedback that he is more emotionally accessible. His relationships with people in and beyond the workplace are deeper and more vulnerable. He is experiencing the transformation of being a different leader from the inside out. And as he is continuing to grow, so is his company.

Recently, he was asked to speak to his sales team at their conference, something he had done in the past. His previous talks had been number-crunchers: *Here is where we are and where we should be going, given the current trends.* But this time, he tried something different. He spoke about the power of emotional vulnerability in the sales world. He mentioned how transformative a conversation can be when it is engaged in with transparency.

Terry was a bit nervous about how his talk would be received, as he was known as a numbers guy. But when he was done, people told him it was the best talk they had ever heard him give.

Terry's transformation illustrates the foundational principle of this book: *If you pay attention to and develop your gut, it will not let you down.*

That is why leading from your gut is key to your efforts. The more you are involved in both the hard and the soft data, the better equipped you will be to execute your tasks and responsibilities. Your values, your emotions, your relationships, and the other aspects of your inner world can help you focus on the important, recruit and train the best people, and find and follow the greatest opportunities.

Looking inward as well as outward may at first feel like a counter-intuitive process. Leaders more naturally turn to the next step, the next meeting, the next idea. But leading from the gut is a habit that can be learned with persistence. Here are a few recommendations to help.

Get connected to others who value the inside world. Interacting with people who are also harnessing the power of their inner world will help you normalize the practice of looking inside as part of leadership. It will form a part of your life. While these people might ideally also be leaders, it is not necessary. Find people who are growing, safe, and interested in values, thoughts, emotions, relationships, and transformation. This creates a culture and a way of looking at life and leadership that works.

Become inaccessible at regular times. Set aside regular times when you step away from meetings, phones, texts, and e-mails for a period and pay attention to what is going on inside you. Your inside world is not generally attention seeking. It is designed to work for you when you seek it out. If the external distractions are too powerful, you will not be able to hear the still, small voice of your creativity, for example, or recognize an important value you have. This doesn't always have to be a long time, it could be just a few minutes. There is information and help available and waiting for you.

Tie the work to the outcomes. Reaching inside yourself, facing your emotions, and taking relational risks all involve effort. And leaders understand that every effort must create a benefit that moves the mission along; otherwise, they stop doing it and replace it with something else that creates a benefit. I hope you have seen the many examples in this book in which doing the tasks of leading from the gut moves you, your people, and your organization toward the goals you are banded together to accomplish.

Pay attention to what happens to your goals, quotas, statistics, results, profits, revenues, and all outcome measures. Using your internal life to help you focus on the right things, think clearly, pay attention to emotional signals, draw on your relational abilities, and work out a better you in your growth context, should, all things being equal, bear you better leadership fruit. That is the hope. It is backed up by research and by reality itself.

I hope you will experience that both worlds—leadership with reason and leadership with your gut—will help you both professionally and personally. Ultimately, leadership from the gut is about life from the gut. It transcends your leadership and your work and is a central part of who you are and the people you are in contact with. In that sense, to the extent that you are aware of and responsive to your interior world, you are also becoming a better and more fulfilled person.

My best to you.

John Townsend
Newport Beach, California
January 2018

NOTES

Chapter 1: Harnessing Your Intuition

1. Daniel Goleman, Richard E. Boyatzis, and Annie McKee, *Primal Leadership: Realizing the Power of Emotional Intelligence* (Boston: Harvard Business School Press, 2002).

Chapter 2: What Are Values?

1. I suggest you have no fewer than three core values, because it's hard to have enough depth otherwise; and no more than seven, because our brains get tired with long lists!

2. James O'Toole, *Leading Change: The Argument for Values-Based Leadership* (New York: Ballentine, 1995), 7.

3. Henry Cloud, *Integrity: The Courage to Meet the Demands of Reality* (New York: HarperCollins, 2006).

Part II: Thoughts: Leaders Think about Thinking

1. For additional information, see John Dunlosky and Janet Metcalf, *Metacognition* (Thousand Oaks, CA: SAGE, 2008).

Chapter 4: Your Heart Has a Brain

1. To find out if *New Life Live!* is playing in your area, visit www.newlife. com.

Chapter 5: Your Mind Has a Gut

1. Malcolm Gladwell, *Blink: The Power of Thinking without Thinking* (New York: Little, Brown and Company, 2005); David G Myers, *Intuition: Its Powers and Perils* (New Haven, CT: Yale University Press, 2002).

2. Marcus Buckingham's writing on clarity has been a major contribution to helping people recognize how important it is for leaders to think clearly and to give clarity to those they lead. For more information about clarity in leadership, see his book *The One Thing You Need to Know* (New York: Free Press, 2005).

3. For more information about cognitive distortions, see David D. Burns, *The Feeling Good Handbook: Using the New Mood Therapy in Everyday Life* (New York: William Morrow, 1989).

4. Keith Sawyer, *Explaining Creativity: The Science of Human Innovation* (New York: Oxford Press, 2006).

5. DVDs and related materials available at www.growthskills.org.

6. Karen Horney, *The Unknown Karen Horney: Essays on Gender, Culture, and Psychoanalysis*, ed., Bernard J. Paris (New Haven, CT: Yale University Press, 2000), 335.

Chapter 6: Harnessing Both Negative and Positive Emotions for Leadership

1. For more information on Ultimate Leadership Workshops, see www.cloudtownsend.com.

Chapter 7: The Pursuit of Passion

1. It's important not to confuse leadership *passion* with leadership *vision*. Passion is an intense, positive feeling focused on an object. Vision is an emotionally compelling picture of what you want the future to be.

2. Robert Frost, "The Road Not Taken," 1916.

Chapter 8: Relational Images

1. For additional guidance on this, see Henry Cloud and John Townsend, *Safe People* (Grand Rapids: Zondervan, 1996).

2. For additional guidance on forgiveness, see chapter 6, "Letting Go," in my book *Loving People* (Nashville: Nelson, 2010).

Chapter 9: Relational Abilities

1. For additional guidance, see Henry Cloud and John Townsend, *How to Have That Difficult Conversation You've Been Avoiding* (Grand Rapids: Zondervan, 2006).

Part V: Transformation: Growing as a Leader

1. Robert Klara, "Infographic: A Look at the Millions of Lives Saved and Improved by the Gates Foundation," *Adweek* (www.adweek.com), June 1, 2016.
2. Julie Bort, "Bill Gates Talks about the Heartbreaking Moment that Turned Him to Philanthropy," *Business Insider* (businessinsider.com), January 21, 2015.

Chapter 10: Personal Growth Is Leadership Growth

1. Bernard Bass and Ronald Riggio, *Transformational Leadership* (Mahwah, NJ: Lawrence Erlbaum Associates, 2005).
2. It's also important to note that transformation is not about skill building. Competencies, vision casting, people management, and strengths building are all necessary parts of leadership training and development. They are the skills you need to develop the right culture, the right people, and the right results. But the focus here is on what you need to grow and develop as a person, in your own character.
3. For additional guidance about how to deal successfully with people who have a low level of ownership in their lives, see James Burns, *Transforming Leadership* (New York: Grove Press, 2003); John Townsend, *Who's Pushing Your Buttons?* (Nashville: Thomas Nelson, 2005).
4. Peter Drucker, *The Effective Executive* (New York: HarperCollins, 1967), 71–99.
5. Marcus Buckingham and Donald Clifton, *Now, Discover Your Strengths* (New York: Free Press, 2001).

Chapter 11: Spiritual Growth Is Leadership Growth

1. *Ryrie Study Bible*, note for 1 Corinthians 2:15 (Chicago: Moody Press, 1978), 1730.
2. Henry Cloud and John Townsend, *How People Grow: What the Bible Reveals about Personal Growth* (Grand Rapids: Zondervan, 2001), 192–93.

ABOUT DR. JOHN TOWNSEND

Dr. John Townsend is a *New York Times* bestselling author, business consultant, leadership coach, and psychologist. He has written over thirty books, selling 10 million copies, including the *Boundaries* series and *The Entitlement Cure*.

For more than twenty years, Dr. Townsend has engaged with leaders, organizations, and individuals around the globe, offering them life-changing solutions to their problems. He is a cohost of the nationally syndicated talk show *New Life Live!* which is heard in 180 markets with three million listeners.

John has created TownsendNOW (townsendnow.com), which delivers both digital content for personal growth and leadership, as well as live digital experiences for growth such as RolePLAY and LaserCOACH.

Dr. Townsend is founder of the Townsend Institute for Leadership and Counseling, which offers graduate degrees and credentialing in Organizational Leadership, Executive Coaching, and Counseling. He is the Clinical Director of the American Association of Christian Counselors.

John formed the Townsend Leadership Program, which develops leaders nationwide, conducted by a team of directors who have been personally trained by John. In addition, John's team, the Townsend Leadership Group, consults with organizations and provides executive coaching services.

Dr. Townsend works personally with leaders and organizations by providing team and executive coaching, corporate consulting, and by giving conference presentations. He also coaches families, and family businesses.

John also speaks at, and supports, GrowthSkills (growthskills.org), a one-week breakthrough growth intensive for leaders, counselors, and those wishing to grow.

John is active on several boards, including Mustard Seed Ranch, a residential program for abused children. A resident of Newport Beach, California, Dr. Townsend and his wife, Barbi, have two grown sons, Ricky and Benny. One of John's passions is playing in a band, which performs at Southern California lounges and venues.

Contact information:
john@drtownsend.com
TownsendNOW.com
drtownsend.com
townsendinstitute.org
facebook.com/drtownsendspage
llinkedin.com/in/drjohntownsend
growthskills.org
949-249-2398